SA1
ROMAN CALENDAR

Including the National Calendars
of Australia, England, Ireland, Scotland & Wales

by Fr Nicholas Schofield

*All booklets are published thanks to the
generous support of the members of the
Catholic Truth Society*

CATHOLIC TRUTH SOCIETY

PUBLISHERS TO THE HOLY SEE

TABLE OF CONTENTS

KEY

The majority of Saints and Blesseds referred to in the text are part of the General Roman Calender, the rank of feast is given in red underneath the Saint's name. To differentiate solemnities, feasts and memorials which belong to National Calendars and are thus celebrated only in a particular territory, or whose rank is different in that territory, a red line is placed before and after. Where various national feasts are celebrated on a given day, these are divided by a short red line and ordered according to rank and then alphabetically by territory.

INTRODUCTION

Scattered across the liturgical year, interwoven through the seasons, are the feasts of the saints. As can be seen by flicking through the pages of the Roman Martyrology, the official book listing these anniversaries, every day of the year is dedicated to the memory of saints who lived in diverse times, places and conditions. The dates chosen are typically that of the saint's death (*dies natalis*), burial (*dies depositionis*) or translation of the relics. In the case of Our Lady and St John the Baptist the date of their earthly birthday is also marked year by year. In some instances another significant day is chosen: thus, Blessed John Henry Newman is commemorated on the anniversary of his reception into the Church. The resulting 'sanctoral cycle' presents us with a rich cloud of witnesses who continue to inspire us and intercede on our behalf.

The saints fulfill several functions in the life of the Church. They are 'historical witnesses to the universal vocation to holiness,' 'illustrious disciples of Christ,' 'citizens of the heavenly Jerusalem who ceaselessly sing the glory and mercy of God,' 'intercessors and friends of the faithful who are still on the earthly pilgrimage' and patrons of particular places, professions and circumstances.[1] The Catechism of the Catholic Church goes on to describe them as 'guides for prayer,' not only because of their heavenly intercession but the personal

---

[1] *Directory on Popular Piety* 211

charisms or 'spiritualities' which they have handed on, 'so that their followers may have a share in this spirit.'[2]

Many traditions and customs have developed over the centuries but 'the ultimate object of veneration of the Saints is the glory of God and the sanctification of man by conforming one's life fully to the divine will and by imitating the virtue of those who were pre-eminent disciples of the Lord.'[3] The cult of the saints, despite the claims of some of its detractors, is always Christocentric - centred on Christ.

Within the Church's Calendar there are various distinctions, which can seem complicated to the uninitiated. Celebrations are ranked as Solemnities (some of which are Holydays of Obligation), Feasts, Obligatory Memorials and Optional Memorials. There are also different types of Calendar. The Universal Calendar is observed by Catholics everywhere and includes saints deemed to be of global significance, such as the apostles, notable martyrs and virgins, and Doctors of the Church. Other Calendars apply to particular regions (for example, the Patrons of Europe), nations or localities (as with the diocesan Calendars or patrons of a particular parish). Added to this are the Calendars of the various religious orders and congregations, which are followed in their respective houses, parishes and institutions.

This booklet is not meant to be a comprehensive dictionary of saints; these are readily available elsewhere.

---

[2] *CCC* 2684
[3] *Directory on Popular Piety* 212

Rather these brief biographies are intended to be a companion to the liturgical year and an aid to prayer. They originally appeared in the Daily Missal published by the Catholic Truth Society and are here presented in a more convenient format. If thought appropriate, the texts could be used by the celebrant at the beginning of Mass or even in the homily. In summarising the lives of the saints, an effort has been made to provide only the essential details and to avoid anything that is historically dubious.

The saints covered in these pages are those in the universal calendar as well as those celebrated nationally in Australia, England and Wales, Ireland and Scotland. Some of these 'local' saints are figures of considerable obscurity. Even their dates, names and life stories are the subject of scholarly debate. Nevertheless they are commemorated by the Church because in many cases they evangelised whole areas or dioceses. They are truly our fathers in faith and friends in Heaven.

Fr Nicholas Schofield

JANUARY

1 January: Octave of Christmas
Solemnity of Mary,
the Holy Mother of God

As we start a new calendar year, the Church celebrates Mary's title as Theotokos, 'God-bearer', defined by the Council of Ephesus (431). Mary is the Mother of Jesus Christ, true God and true man; hence she is the 'Mother of God'. She brought Jesus into the world and continues to bring people to Him, 'to Jesus through Mary.' She is indeed the Mother of the Church and we are called to share in her Motherhood. As St Bernard wrote: 'what use would it be to me that Christ was born once of Mary in Bethlehem if he were not born of faith in my soul too?'

2 January
Saints Basil the Great and Gregory Nazianzen
Bishops and Doctors of the Church
Memorial

St Basil (c.330-379) was born into a saintly family in Caesarea, Cappadocia (Turkey); his brother was St Gregory of Nyssa, also a notable theologian. For some years St Basil lived in a monastic community before becoming Bishop of Caesarea in 370. He was a keen defender of the reality of the Incarnation against attacks from Arian heretics. St Basil also gave his name to a Liturgy and a set of monastic rules which are still used in the East.

St Gregory Nazianzen (330-390), a friend of St Basil, was also from Cappadocia and involved in countering the Arian heresy.

In 381 he became Bishop of Constantinople, although he had to retire to his native Nazianzus due to opposition. He was called 'The Theologian' because of his great learning and talent for oratory.

3 January

The Most Holy Name of Jesus

Optional Memorial

On the day of his Circumcision the Lord received the name Jesus, meaning 'God saves.' Devotion to the Holy Name was popularised in the fifteenth century by St Bernardine of Siena and St John Capistrano, who both carried the monogram of Jesus (IHS) with them on their preaching tours. We honour the Holy Name not only because it is the name of our Saviour but because it is, in itself, a powerful prayer.

In Ireland

Saint Munchin, Bishop

Optional Memorial

St Munchin or Mainchín (seventh century?), possibly of royal blood, is venerated as founder of the Church in Limerick. He may have been its first bishop. Little is known for certain of his life.

---

7 January

Saint Raymond of Penyafort, Priest

Optional Memorial

St Raymond (c.1175-1275) belonged to a noble Catalonian family and joined the Dominican Order. He worked for many years in Rome, codifying Canon Law in five books of Decretals, and in 1238 became the Order's third Master-General. He is particularly remembered for promoting the fruitful celebration of the Sacrament of Penance and for his compassion towards Christian slaves.

In England

12 January

Saint Aelred of Rievaulx

Optional Memorial

St Aelred (1109-1167) was born at Hexham and joined the Cistercian monastery of Rievaulx in Yorkshire. He served as Abbot at Revesby, Lincolnshire, and Rievaulx, and became known as a preacher and writer, the 'Bernard of the North.' He delighted in friendship and wrote: 'he who dwells in friendship, dwells in God and God in him.'

---

13 January

Saint Hilary, Bishop and Doctor of the Church

Optional Memorial

St Hilary (c.315-368) was brought up a pagan and married young. He later converted to Christianity and, as Bishop of Poitiers, was a leading defender of the Church against the Arian heresy, which caused him to be exiled to Phrygia by the Arian emperor Constantius. He was declared a Doctor of the Church in 1851.

In Scotland

Saint Kentigern, Bishop

Feast

Little is known for certain about St Kentigern (whose nickname was Mungo). Legend has it that he established a community of monks near what is now Glasgow and was consecrated a bishop, before political disagreements led to his exile in Cumbria or possibly Wales, though he later returned to Glasgow. He died around 612. A cathedral was built over his tomb and his various reputed miracles are represented in the city's coat of arms.

In Ireland

15 January

Saint Ita, Virgin

Memorial

Little is known for certain about St Ita (+ c.570). Later legends say she was born in Drum, County Waterford, led a female community at Killeedy, County Limerick, and that she was famous for her penances and miracles. Her monastery ran a school that is said to have educated many other Irish saints.

In Ireland

16 January

Saint Fursa, Abbot and Missionary

Optional Memorial

St Fursa or Fursey (+ c.648) was born in Connaught and reputedly baptised by St Brendan. Entering the monastic life, he established monasteries in Ireland (Rathmat), England (Burgh Castle, Norfolk) and France (Lagny, near Paris). He died at Mézerolles in northern France and was buried at nearby Péronne on the Somme.

---

17 January
Saint Anthony, Abbot
Memorial

St Anthony (c.251-356) was born into a wealthy family but retired into the Egyptian desert at the age of eighteen. Having faced numerous temptations, he formed a community and counselled those who came to him, including St Athanasius, who wrote his Life. He is honoured as the Patriarch of Monks.

In England

19 January
Saint Wulstan, Bishop
Memorial

St Wulfstan or Wulstan (1008-1095) became a Benedictine monk at Worcester and, after serving as Precentor and Prior, was appointed Bishop in 1062. He was the only Englishman to retain his see after the Norman Conquest. His wise and benevolent rule lasted thirty-two years, during which he rebuilt his cathedral, reformed the diocese and tried to stop the slave-trade at Bristol. English slaves were sold to Norse traders in Ireland until the twelfth century.

---

20 January
Saint Fabian, Pope and Martyr
Optional Memorial

St Fabian (+ 250) was elected Bishop of Rome in 236, despite not being in Holy Orders. He divided Rome into seven deaconries for the purpose of extending aid to the poor and was finally martyred under the Emperor Decius. St Cyprian called him an 'incomparable man.'

Saint Sebastian, Martyr

Optional Memorial

St Sebastian (+ c.300) came from Milan and, according to legend, was an officer in Diocletian's imperial guard. After becoming a Christian, he suffered martyrdom in Rome and his tomb on the Via Appia was soon visited by pilgrims. He is often shown in art transfixed with arrows and is a patron of doctors and policemen.

21 January

Saint Agnes, Virgin and Martyr

Memorial

St Agnes (+ c.304) came from a noble Roman family. According to a fifth century Life, she was about thirteen years old when she suffered martyrdom by being stabbed in the throat, after refusing to be married to a pagan. She was buried on the Via Nomentana and her name is included in the Roman Canon. She is often shown with a lamb, a symbol of her purity and also a play on her name (which in Greek means 'chaste') and the Latin word agnus (meaning 'lamb').

22 January

Saint Vincent, Deacon and Martyr

Memorial

St Vincent (+ 304) was a deacon of the Church in Saragossa, Spain. He was brutally tortured and martyred at Valencia in the persecution under Diocletian. His cult grew quickly and both St Augustine and St Leo preached sermons in his honour. He is the proto-martyr of Spain.

24 January

Saint Francis de Sales, Bishop and Doctor of the Church

Memorial

St Francis de Sales (1567-1622) was born in Thorens, Savoy (France) and trained as a lawyer before being ordained. He became Bishop of Geneva in 1602 and did much to combat Calvinism. He also founded the Order of the Visitation, with St Jane Frances de Chantal, and produced popular spiritual works such as Introduction to the Devout Life. His flock called him 'the Gentle Christ of Geneva'. Pius XI declared St Francis patron of journalists and writers in 1923.

25 January

The Conversion of Saint Paul the Apostle

Feast

This Feast commemorates the conversion of Saul of Tarsus while he was on his way to Damascus to persecute Christians. He was blinded by a light and thrown from his horse to the ground, hearing the words, 'Saul, Saul, why do you persecute me?' As Pope Benedict XVI wrote, 'the Risen One spoke to Paul, called him to the apostolate and made him a true Apostle, a witness of the Resurrection, with the specific task of proclaiming the Gospel to the Gentiles, to the Graeco-Roman world.'

26 January
Saints Timothy and Titus, Bishops

Memorial

SS Timothy and Titus were both apostles of St Paul, who addressed to them three of his Epistles. St Timothy (+ 97) accompanied the Apostle on many of his journeys and eventually became bishop of Ephesus. According to tradition, he was beaten to death by a mob when he opposed the worship of Dionysus.

St Titus (+ c.96) seems to have served as the first bishop of Crete.

In Australia: Optional Memorial

27 January
Saints Timothy and Titus, Bishops

See 26 January.

Saint Angela Merici, Virgin

Optional Memorial

St Angela Merici (1474-1540) was born near Verona, Italy, and devoted herself to the education of girls and the care of the sick. In 1516 she founded the Institute of St Ursula (Ursulines), the first teaching order for women approved by the Church.

28 January
Saint Thomas Aquinas,
Priest and Doctor of the Church

Memorial

St Thomas Aquinas (c.1224-1274) was a Dominican friar who became one of the most important Christian philosophers and theologians. Known as the 'Angelic Doctor', he had an astonishing mastery of scholastic theology and a profound holiness of life. His greatest work, the Summa Theologica, is still widely used. Pope Leo XIII declared him patron of Catholic schools.

In Ireland

30 January
Saint Aidan, Bishop
Optional Memorial

St Aidan or Máedóc (+ 626), not to be confused with St Aidan of Lindisfarne, was born in Inisbrefny, County Cavan, and was a monk under St David in Wales. He became the first Bishop of Ferns, County Wexford and founded a number of monasteries, including those at Fernes and his birthplace of Inisbrefny.

---

31 January
Saint John Bosco, Priest
Memorial

St John Bosco (1815-1888) was born in Piedmont (Italy) and devoted his life to Catholic education. This 'Apostle of Youth' founded the Salesian Order, named in honour of St Francis de Sales, and, with the help of St Mary Mazzarello, the Daughters of Mary Help of Christians. Despite meeting much opposition, his aim was, above all, to educate through love.

FEBRUARY

1 February

Saint Brigid, Abbess,
Secondary Patron of Ireland

Feast

St Brigid or Bride (+ c.525), is known as 'the Mary of the Gael'. Details of her life are obscure; she was supposedly born near Dundalk, County Louth, entered the religious life, and later founded a double community at Kildare, which soon became an episcopal see with St Conleth as its first bishop. She was famous for her works of charity and widely venerated in Ireland and beyond.

2 February

The Presentation of the Lord

Feast

The Presentation of the Lord, popularly known as 'Candlemas,' traditionally concludes the celebration of Christmas. It commemorates the presentation of Jesus in the Temple forty days after his birth, an occasion when offerings were made and the mother was ritually purified. Simeon's prophecy referred to Jesus as 'a light to enlighten the pagans', summing up the Christmas theme of light coming into the darkness, but also points towards the Paschal Mystery, for He was 'destined to be a sign that is rejected.'

3 February
Saint Blaise, Bishop and Martyr
Optional Memorial

St Blaise (+ c.316) was bishop of Sebaste in Armenia. He was martyred under Licinius. Cures were attributed to him and it is the custom in many places to bless throats on his feast.

Saint Ansgar, Bishop
Optional Memorial

St Ansgar or Anskar (801-865) was a French Benedictine monk who is known as the 'Apostle of the North'. As Archbishop of Hamburg and Papal Legate, he worked for thirteen years preaching the gospel in northern Germany, Denmark and Sweden. The saint laid the foundations of the Church in these places, even though there were later relapses into paganism.

5 February
Saint Agatha, Virgin and Martyr
Memorial

St Agatha (+ 251) suffered martyrdom at Catania in Sicily, probably during the time of Decius. According to a later Life, the tortures she was subjected to included cutting off her breasts, which have become her symbol in art. She was widely venerated as a martyr and her name appears in the Roman Canon.

6 February
Saint Paul Miki and Companions, Martyrs
Memorial

St Paul Miki and his twenty-five companions were martyred in Nagasaki, Japan in 1597. They were crucified and then stabbed with spears, though the executioners were astounded upon seeing their joy at being thus associated with the passion of Christ. They were the first martyrs of the Far East to be canonised.

In Ireland

7 February

Saint Mel, Bishop

Optional Memorial

St Mel (+ c.490) is said to have been a nephew or disciple of St Patrick, joining him as a missionary in Ireland. He eventually became first bishop of Ardagh and is venerated as the patron of the diocese of Ardagh and Clonmacnoise.

8 February

Saint Jerome Emiliani

Optional Memorial

St Jerome Emiliani (1486-1537) was born in Venice and led a dissolute youth. Serving as a soldier, he was taken captive but attributed his liberation to the intercession of Our Lady. Henceforth he dedicated himself to a life of charity. He founded a congregation of clerks regular known as the Somaschi, dedicated to the education of children, especially orphans. He died of the plague in 1537 while caring for the afflicted. In 1928 he was named patron of orphans and abandoned children.

Saint Josephine Bakhita, Virgin

Optional Memorial

St Josephine Bakhita (c.1868-1947) was born in the Darfur region of the Sudan and spent much of her early life as a slave. She eventually settled in Italy, where she converted to

Christianity and entered the Canossian Daughters of Charity at Schio, near Vicenza. Serving quietly as the community's portress, cook and sacristan, she gained a reputation for exceptional piety and holiness.

In Wales

9 February

Saint Teilo, Bishop

Optional Memorial

St Teilo (sixth century) was probably born near Penally, Pembrokeshire. He founded the important monastery at Llandeilo Fawr; later legend has him spending time in Brittany, and makes him bishop of Llandaff. He is widely venerated in Wales and Brittany.

---

10 February

Saint Scholastica, Virgin

Memorial

St Scholastica (+ c.543) was the sister of St Benedict. She followed the rule of her brother near Montecassino and is regarded as the first Benedictine nun. When she met her brother for the last time, a sudden rainstorm providentially prolonged the meeting; three days later St Benedict saw her soul ascend to heaven as a dove (her symbol in art).

11 February

Our Lady of Lourdes

Optional Memorial

The feast marks the first apparition of the Blessed Virgin Mary in 1858 to fourteen-year-old St Bernadette Soubirous.

There were eighteen apparitions in all, the last of which was on 16 July 1858. The message of Lourdes is a call to personal conversion, prayer and charity. In a special way, the shrine has become closely associated with the sick.

In Ireland

Saint Gobnait, Virgin

Optional Memorial

St Gobnait or Gobnet (sixth century) was probably born in County Clare and, according to legend, studied with St Enda on the Aran Islands. Medieval sources claim she founded churches at Dunquin, County Kerry and Dungarvan, County Waterford and a monastery at Ballyvourney, County Cork. She is remembered for her love of bee-keeping and her care of the sick.

---

14 February

Saints Cyril, Monk, and Methodius, Bishop
Patrons of Europe

Memorial (In Europe: Feast)

These two brothers evangelised Moravia, Bohemia, and Bulgaria and are venerated as the 'Apostles of the Slavs.' They translated liturgical books into Slavonic with the help of the Cyrillic alphabet, which they invented. St Cyril (+ 869) died in Rome where he had gone to seek the Pope's blessing. St Methodius (+ 885) was consecrated a bishop and ended his days in Pannonia (Hungary). Blessed John Paul II proclaimed them Patrons of Europe, along with St Benedict.

17 February
The Seven Holy Founders of the Servite Order
Optional Memorial

The 'Seven Holy Founders' were members of the Confraternity of Our Lady in Florence who withdrew to live the eremitical life on Monte Senario in 1233. They founded the Servants of Mary (Servite Friars), which received papal approval in 1304. The Servites led an austere life of prayer and mortification, meditating constantly on the Lord's Passion and venerating Our Lady of Sorrows.

In Ireland
Saint Fintan, Abbot
Optional Memorial

St Fintan (+ c.603) was born in Leinster and lived as a hermit at Clonenagh in Leix. Despite the austerity of his life, he attracted many disciples and founded a large monastery at Clonenagh.

21 February
Saint Peter Damian, Bishop and Doctor of the Church
Optional Memorial

St Peter Damian (1007-1072) was born at Ravenna and joined the monastic community at Fonte Avellana, founded by St Romuald. Having served as Abbot, St Peter was created Cardinal Bishop of Ostia in 1057 and took a leading part in Church reform. An important theologian and poet, he was declared a Doctor of the Church in 1828.

22 February

The Chair of Saint Peter the Apostle

Feast

The celebration of the Cathedra Petri, the Chair of St Peter, recalls the ministry conferred by Christ on the Prince of the Apostles and continued in an unbroken line down to the present Pope. It is an opportunity for the faithful to renew their communion with the Roman Pontiff and to follow closely his teachings.

23 February

Saint Polycarp, Bishop and Martyr

Memorial

St Polycarp (+ c.155) was converted to Christianity by St John the Evangelist. He was later ordained bishop of Smyrna (now Izmir, Turkey). As an old man he was urged by the Roman proconsul to renounce Christ in order to save his life. The saint replied, 'For eighty-six years I have served him and he has never wronged me. How can I renounce the King who has saved me?' He was executed and his body burnt; his followers collected his relics and wrote an account of his life and martyrdom.

MARCH

1 March

Saint David, Bishop, Patron of Wales

In Wales: Solemnity; In England: Feast

St David (+ c.600) was born in south Wales. We know little of his life; tradition says he founded a monastery at Mynyw (Menevia) and was consecrated bishop (according to legend in Jerusalem). He lived an austere life. Many Welsh monasteries claimed him as founder. His cult spread quickly and in 1120 Pope Callistus II declared that two pilgrimages to his shrine at St Davids were equivalent to one to Rome.

4 March

Saint Casimir

Optional Memorial

St Casimir (1458-1484) was the third son of King Casimir IV of Poland. A shining example of faith, piety, humility, and chastity, he had little interest in proposals to arrange an advantageous marriage, and refused to go to war against other Christian princes. His devotion to Our Lady was great; he was so fond of the twelfth-century hymn 'Daily, daily sing to Mary' that it is often attributed to him. He died of tuberculosis aged twenty-six and was named patron of Poland in 1602.

In Ireland

5 March

Saint Kieran, Bishop

Optional Memorial

St Kieran or Ciaran (+ c.530), known as 'the first-born of the saints of Ireland' and one of the 'Twelve Apostles of Ireland,' came from Ossory. Some say he predated St Patrick, others that he was consecrated bishop by him. He lived for a time as a hermit and, according to tradition, his first disciples were animals of the woods. He soon attracted human disciples and a monastery and town developed at Saighir. St Kieran is the patron of the diocese of Ossory.

7 March

Saints Perpetua and Felicity, Martyrs

Memorial

St Perpetua, a young mother of noble birth, and St Felicity, a heavily pregnant slave girl, were imprisoned at Carthage in 203 because of their Christian faith. Before they met their death (they were thrown to wild beasts in the arena), Felicity gave birth to a girl; Perpetua was still nursing her new-born son. The Passion of St Perpetua provides a particularly vivid account of their martyrdom. They are included in the Roman Canon.

8 March

Saint John of God, Religious

Optional Memorial

St John of God (1495-1550) was born at Montemor-o-Novo (Portugal) and took a number of employments, including shepherd, soldier and bookseller. Encouraged by St John of Avila, he experienced a conversion of heart aged forty-two and started serving the sick in Granada (Spain). For this purpose, he founded the Brothers Hospitallers (Brothers of St John of God) and is venerated as patron of the sick and of hospitals, and also of booksellers.

In Ireland

Saint Senan, Bishop

Optional Memorial

St Senan (+ c.540) was born near Kilrush, County Clare, and entered the monastic life at Kilmanagh in Ossory. St Senan established several monasteries, including the one on Scattery Island, where he was eventually buried.

---

9 March

Saint Frances of Rome, Religious

Optional Memorial

St Frances of Rome (1384-1440) was a married woman and mother of six children. She patiently endured many trials, including the death of two of her children, the exile of her husband and the confiscation of their estates. In 1433 she founded the Benedictine Oblates of the Tor de'Specchi to continue her works of charity, and after her husband died in 1436 she became their superior. She often saw her guardian angel at her side, guiding and protecting her, which may be why she was named patron of motorists by Pope Pius XI.

In Scotland

10 March
Saint John Ogilvie, Martyr
Feast

St John Ogilvie (1580-1615) was born at Drum-na-Keith, Banffshire, and raised as a Calvinist. After being received into the Church at Louvain in 1596, he joined the Society of Jesus. He returned to Scotland in 1613 but was betrayed and captured after only nine months. On 10 March 1615 he was hanged at Glasgow.

In Ireland

11 March
Saint Aengus, Bishop and Abbot
Optional Memorial

St Aengus or Tengus (+ c.830) was a monk of Clonenagh and later Tallaght. He is famous for writing an early metrical martyrology, the Félire Tengusso ('Martyrology of Tengus'). He may have been ordained bishop.

17 March
Saint Patrick, Bishop, Patron of Ireland
Optional Memorial (In Ireland & Australia: Solemnity; In England and Scotland: Feast)

St Patrick (385-461) was born into a Christian Romano-British family. His first encounter with Ireland was as a slave after he was captured by raiders at the age of sixteen. After escaping, he probably studied in Gaul and was ordained a priest. Around 432 he returned to Ireland as a missionary bishop and succeeded in consolidating the faith in large parts of the country.

18 March

Saint Cyril of Jerusalem, Bishop and Doctor of the Church

Optional Memorial

St Cyril (c.315-387) was born near Jerusalem and for many years served as Patriarch of that holy city, although disputes with heretics and others forced him to live in exile for seventeen years. He is best known for his catechetical instructions, which led him to be declared a Doctor of the Church in 1882.

19 March

Saint Joseph, Spouse of the Blessed Virgin Mary

Solemnity

Not a single word of his is recorded in Sacred Scripture and yet St Joseph is one of the greatest and most popular saints, largely because of his humility and his closeness to Our Lord. He died before the beginning of Jesus's public ministry and, since he probably died in the presence of Jesus and Mary, is venerated as the patron of a good death. Blessed Pius IX named him patron of the universal church and Blessed John XXIII added his name to the Roman Canon.

In Ireland

21 March

Saint Enda, Abbot

Optional Memorial

St Enda (+ c.530) may have been a disciple of St Ninian and founded the first Irish monastery on Aran, 'the capital of the Ireland of the saints.' It had a great influence on the Irish

Church and, according to St Aengus, 'it will never be known
until the day of judgement the number of saints whose bodies
lie in the soil of Aran.'

23 March
Saint Turibius of Mogrovejo, Bishop
Optional Memorial

St Turibius of Mongrovejo (1538-1606) was born at Mayorga
(Spain) and worked for many years as Professor of Law at
Salamanca. In 1580, even though he was a layman, he was
appointed archbishop of Lima (Peru), where, after being
ordained, he did much to consolidate ecclesiastical discipline
and champion the rights of indigenous peoples.

In Ireland

24 March
Saint Macartan, Bishop
Optional Memorial

St Macartan (+ c.505) was reputedly a disciple of St Patrick and
first bishop of Clogher, County Tyrone. He was known for
his many miracles and is venerated as patron of the Diocese
of Clogher.

25 March
The Annunciation Of The Lord
Solemnity

On the floor of the Holy House in Nazareth, an inscription
reads 'Verbum caro hic factum est'; 'the Word was made flesh
here'. When the Blessed Virgin said 'yes' to the Angel Gabriel,

the Word became flesh and dwelt in her womb for nine months. The Annunciation is the prologue to the mysteries of Holy Week: the Incarnation happened so that we could be redeemed; the child conceived on this day was born to die for our sins and conquer death.

APRIL

1 April

Saint Ceallach (Celsus), Bishop

Optional Memorial

St Ceallach or Celsus (1079-1129) became Archbishop of Armagh as a twenty-six year-old layman, inheriting it as a family fief. He was referred to by St Bernard as a 'worthy and God-fearing man,' and promoted the reform of the Church through visitations and synods, despite facing much opposition. He appointed St Malachy as his successor, thus breaking the hereditary right to the See held by his own family. He was buried at Lismore, County Waterford.

2 April

Saint Francis of Paola, Hermit

Optional Memorial

St Francis of Paola (1416-1507) initially joined the Franciscans but left to live as a hermit in a cave on the Calabrian coast, near his birthplace, Paola. He was soon joined by others who wished to devote their lives to prayer and penance. The community developed into the Order of Minims (Minimi fratres, the 'least brethren'). After being called to console King Louis XI on his deathbed, St Francis moved to France, where he founded several Minim houses.

4 April

Saint Isidore, Bishop and Doctor of the Church

Optional Memorial

St Isidore (560-636) was born in Seville (Spain) and succeeded his elder brother as Bishop of Seville around the year 600. He did much to consolidate the Spanish Church by calling councils, founding religious houses and fighting Arianism. He was a prolific author; his last work, Etymologies, was an encyclopedia which continued to be used throughout the Middle Ages. St Isidore was declared a Doctor of the Church in 1722.

5 April

Saint Vincent Ferrer, Priest

Optional Memorial

St Vincent Ferrer (1350-1419) was born at Valencia (Spain) to an English father and Spanish mother. He joined the Dominicans and became renowned as an effective preacher among Christians, Jews and Muslims. Many miracles were attributed to him. He died in 1419 while preaching in Brittany and was buried at Vannes.

7 April

Saint John Baptist de la Salle, Priest

Memorial

St John Baptist de la Salle (1651-1719) was born at Rheims (France). He opened free schools for poor children and introduced new teaching methods, earning him the title 'Father of Modern Pedagogy'. He founded the Brothers of the Christian Schools (De La Salle Brothers), which made a great contribution to popular education. He was declared patron of schoolteachers in 1950.

11 April
Saint Stanislaus, Bishop and Martyr
Memorial

St Stanislaus (Stanisław) (1030-1079) became Bishop of Cracow (Poland) in 1072 and championed the liberty of the Church and the dignity of man. He reproached King Bolesław II for his immoral life, and may have plotted his overthrow; in any event, the King himself murdered the bishop while he was offering Mass. Devotion to Stanislaus grew at once, and he was canonised in 1253. St Stanislaus is the patron of Poland.

13 April
Saint Martin I, Pope and Martyr
Optional Memorial

St Martin I (+ 655) was born in Todi (Italy) and elected Pope in 649. He called a Council to condemn the Monothelite heresy, which denied that Christ had two wills. This angered the Byzantine emperor Constans II, who sympathised with the Monothelites, and St Martin was imprisoned then banished to the Crimea where he died, broken by his sufferings. He is venerated as a martyr.

In Ireland
18 April
Saint Laserian, Bishop
Optional Memorial

St Laserian or Molaise (+ 639), one of the 'Twelve Apostles of Ireland'; legend has him born of a royal Ulster family and educated by St Fintan of Taghmon, whom he later opposed over the dating of Easter. He became Abbot of Leighlin, County

Carlow, where he is associated with a holy well. Claims he was ordained a bishop in Rome are unlikely to be true.

In Wales

20 April

Saint Beuno, Abbot

Optional Memorial

St Beuno (+ c.650) was born in Powys and founded several monasteries, including Clynnog Fawr in the Llyn Peninsula. Traditionally many miracles were attributed to him, including the restoration of his niece, St Winifride, to life. He is invoked as a patron of sick animals and epileptics.

---

21 April

Saint Anselm, Bishop and Doctor of the Church

Optional Memorial

St Anselm (1033-1109) was born in Aosta (Italy) and joined the Benedictine monastery at Bec in Normandy. He became Abbot and then, in 1093, Archbishop of Canterbury. He endured periods of exile due to his opposition to William II and Henry I, both of whom threatened the Church's liberty. St Anselm is best remembered as an important theologian and the 'Father of Scholasticism'. He was declared Doctor of the Church in 1720.

23 April

Saint George, Martyr, Patron of England

Optional Memorial (In England: Solemnity)

St George (+ c.303) was martyred in Palestine during the persecution of Diocletian at Diospolis (Lydda, now Lod, near Tel Aviv, Israel), where his tomb can be found. Legend depicts him killing the dragon, a symbol of the triumph over evil. He is the patron saint of several countries and regions, including England.

Saint Adalbert, Bishop and Martyr

Optional Memorial

St Adalbert (c.956-997) belonged to a noble Bohemian family and was appointed Bishop of Prague while still young. Twice he retired to Rome due to opposition and he eventually turned his attentions to missionary work in Poland, Hungary and Pomerania. He was killed by the pagan Prussians in 997.

24 April

Saint Fidelis of Sigmaringen, Priest and Martyr

Optional Memorial

St Fidelis (1578-1622) was born at Sigmaringen (Germany) and, after working as a lawyer, joined the Capuchin Order. He led a life of deep contemplation and showed great generosity to the poor. Sent as a missionary to the Swiss Protestants in the Grisons, he was stabbed to death after preaching at the church in Seewis on 24 April 1622.

25 April

Saint Mark, Evangelist

Feast (In Australia: 26 April)

St Mark (+ c.75), the author of the Gospel bearing his name, is often identified as the young man who ran away when the Lord was arrested. His Gospel gives the teaching and memoirs of St Peter. He joined St Paul and St Barnabas on their first missionary journey and later became St Paul's secretary in Rome. He is thought to have established the Church in Alexandria, and to have died a martyr there.

In Australia: Feast

26 April

Saint Mark, Evangelist

See 25 April.

In Ireland

27 April

Saint Asicus, Bishop

Optional Memorial

St Asicus or Assicus (fifth century): legend makes him a disciple of St Patrick and first Bishop of Elphin, though he is said to have spent a period as a hermit in Donegal Bay. He was skilled in metalwork and his artistic symbol is consequently the anvil.

In Australia: Optional Memorial

Saint Louis Grignion de Montfort, Priest

See 28 April.

---

28 April

Saint Peter Chanel, Priest and Martyr

Optional Memorial (In Australia: Memorial)

St Peter Chanel (1803-1841) was born near Belley (France) and joined the Society of Mary (Marists). He was sent to Oceania to spread the Gospel and stationed himself on the island of Futuna, near Tonga. He initially won the confidence of the island's king, Niuliki, but relations deteriorated, especially after the king's son requested baptism. St Peter was clubbed to death on 28 April 1841. He was canonised in 1954 and is the protomartyr of Oceania.

Saint Louis Grignion de Montfort, Priest

Optional Memorial (In Australia: 27 April)

St Louis Grignon de Montfort (1673-1716) was a French diocesan priest with a great devotion to the Virgin Mary; he was noted for his fervent and enthusiastic preaching and apostolate. He founded an order of missionary priests, the Company of Mary, and a sister order of nuns, the Daughters of Wisdom. He is best known, however, for his book True Devotion to the Blessed Virgin Mary, which like most of his writings was not properly published until the nineteenth century. It proposes that the Christian make a "total consecration" of himself to Jesus through Mary; it has had an immense influence, not least on Blessed John Paul II. St Louis was canonised in 1947.

29 April

Saint Catherine of Siena,
Virgin and Doctor of the Church, Patron of Europe

Memorial (In Europe: Feast)

St Catherine (1347-1380) was born at Siena, one of twenty-five children. At a young age she decided to dedicate herself to the Lord and resist the attempts of her family to find her a suitable husband. She became a Dominican Tertiary and both her writings and her stigmata reveal her intimate union with God. Despite her retired life, St Catherine was actively involved in public affairs and persuaded the pope, Gregory XI, to return to Rome from Avignon. She later tried to unite the Church during the Great Schism and moved to Rome, where she died aged thirty-three. She was proclaimed patroness of Italy in 1939, Doctor of the Church in 1970 and a patron of Europe in 1999.

30 April

Saint Pius V, Pope

Optional Memorial

St Pius V (1504-1572) was born as Michael Ghislieri in Piedmont and joined the Dominican Order. Elected Pope in 1565, he enforced the decrees of the Council of Trent, organised a successful crusade against the Turks, published the Roman Catechism, and revised the Missal and Breviary. He also tried to counter Protestantism, and excommunicated Elizabeth I of England in 1570. Canonised in 1712, he is buried at Santa Maria Maggiore, Rome.

MAY

1 May
Saint Joseph the Worker
Optional Memorial

This feast was instituted in 1955 by Pope Pius XII on a day when labour was celebrated in many countries. Jesus was himself 'the son of the carpenter' and St Joseph presents a wonderful example of how even the most seemingly menial work can be sanctified.

2 May
Saint Athanasius, Bishop and Doctor of the Church
Memorial

St Athanasius (c.296-373) was Bishop of Alexandria (Egypt) for some forty-six years. He became the champion of the faith against Arianism and, as a result, was exiled for seventeen years. He wrote many theological works, and Blessed John Henry Newman later wrote that he was 'a principal instrument after the Apostles by which the sacred truths of Christianity have been conveyed and secured to the world.'

3 May
Saints Philip and James, Apostles
Feast

St Philip (first century) was from Bethsaida and, after being called by the Lord, introduced St Bartholomew to Him. He may have been crucified at Hierapolis in Phrygia, where he had preached the Gospel.

St James 'the Less' (+ c.62) was a cousin of the Lord. As bishop of Jerusalem, he wrote an epistle preserved in the New Testament and, legend says, was eventually martyred by being stoned, and then clubbed to death.

In England

4 May

The English Martyrs

Feast

The Feast celebrates the many men and women who suffered for the Faith in England between 1535 and 1680 and have subsequently been recognised by the Church. These included priests, both secular and religious, as well as laity who were prepared to shelter them, to arrange secret Masses, and to witness to the faith. They came from all ages and backgrounds, and their heroic witness helps us have a greater love for the Church, the Mass and the priesthood.

In Ireland

Saint Conleth, Bishop

Optional Memorial

St Conleth (+ c.519) was a hermit who became first bishop of Kildare, where he worked closely with St Brigid and her community. He is said to have been a keen metalworker and copyist and illuminator of manuscripts.

In Wales

5 May

Saint Asaph, Bishop

Optional Memorial

St Asaph (sixth century) was probably a disciple of St Kentigern who spread the Gospel in the Flintshire area and became a bishop. He was connected to the monastery at Llanelwy, where the Normans created a bishopric named after him.

In Ireland

Blessed Edmund Rice, Religious

Optional Memorial

Blessed Edmund Ignatius Rice (1762-1844) was born in Callan, County Kilkenny and was apprenticed to his uncle, a merchant at Waterford. Following the death of his wife, he discerned a vocation to establish Catholic schools and founded the Presentation Brothers in 1802, which was approved by the Pope in 1820, gave rise to the similar Irish Christian Brothers, and spread around the world. He was beatified by Blessed John Paul II in 1996.

In Ireland

10 May

Saint Comgall, Abbot

Optional Memorial

St Comgall (516-601) was born in Dal Araide, Antrim and went on to become the founding Abbot of Bangor, on Belfast Lough, where his students included St Columbanus. A friend of St Columba, he was famous for his emphasis on study and strict discipline.

12 May
Saints Nereus and Achilleus, Martyrs
Optional Memorial

SS Nereus and Achilleus (second century) were Praetorian soldiers who converted to Christianity and were subsequently martyred. Another tradition suggests they were baptised by St Peter himself and eventually beheaded while in exile at Terracina. An ancient basilica in Rome is dedicated to their memory.

Saint Pancras, Martyr
Optional Memorial

St Pancras (+ c.304) was, according to legend, only fourteen years old when he was martyred during the reign of Diocletian. He was buried on the Via Aurelia and a basilica erected over his tomb. His cult spread quickly. Ancient churches were dedicated to him in Canterbury and London.

13 May
Our Lady of Fatima
Optional Memorial

The Blessed Virgin Mary appeared to three shepherd children at Fatima (Portugal) on the thirteenth day for six consecutive months in 1917. She brought a message of peace and reparation for sin, encouraging devotion to her Immaculate Heart and the recitation of the Holy Rosary.

14 May

Saint Matthias, Apostle

Feast

St Matthias (first century) was chosen by lot to take the place of Judas among the Twelve (Acts 1:15-26). He was present at the first Pentecost and, according to various traditions, went on to preach in Judaea, Cappadocia and Ethiopia. He was martyred possibly by means of the axe or halberd with which he is often depicted in art.

In Ireland

15 May

Saint Carthage, Bishop

Optional Memorial

St Carthage (Carthach) or Mochuda (Mo Chuta, Mochta) (+ c.637). According to late accounts, he was born in County Kerry and spent his youth as a swineherd. He became a monk and eventually abbot and bishop at Rahan, County Offaly. Shortly before his death he was expelled from the monastery, with his monks, possibly in a disagreement over the date of Easter. They settled at Lismore, County Waterford, and he spent his final year as a hermit at nearby Inch, on the river Blackwater. He is a patron of the Diocese of Waterford and Lismore.

In Ireland

16 May

Saint Brendan, Abbot

Optional Memorial

St Brendan (c.486-575), one of the 'Twelve Apostles of Ireland,' was born near Tralee and entered the monastic life, founding monasteries at Clonfert, Annadown, Inishadroun and Ardfert. He was also known as having travelled extensively. A ninth century legend records a remarkable journey he is said to have made, with a group of monks, across the Atlantic Ocean to the 'Promised Land of the Saints', identified by some as North America; others interpret the tale as a pure fantastical romance. At any rate, the story was immensely popular, and Irish monks did indeed bring the Gospel to all corners of the earth.

---

18 May

Saint John I, Pope and Martyr

Optional Memorial

St John I (+ 526) was an elderly archdeacon at the time of his election as Bishop of Rome in 523. His brief pontificate was caught up in the violent politics of the age. He was sent by the Gothic King of Italy, Theodoric, who was an Arian heretic, on a mission to Byzantium to secure mutual toleration between Catholics and Arians, and to try to bring the Eastern and Western Churches closer together. Theodoric suspected him of conspiring with the eastern Emperor and imprisoned him. St John died shortly afterwards and is venerated as a martyr.

In England

19 May

Saint Dunstan, Bishop

Optional Memorial

St Dunstan (909-988) belonged to a noble family and served as abbot of Glastonbury (Somerset) and Bishop of Worcester and London and finally Archbishop of Canterbury. He was zealous in building churches, promoting monastic life and restoring ecclesiastical discipline. He was buried at Canterbury Cathedral.

---

20 May
Saint Bernardine of Siena, Priest
Optional Memorial

St Bernardine of Siena (1380-1444) was born in the Republic of Siena (Italy) and entered the Franciscan Order. He became a popular and effective preacher, doing much to convert sinners and spread devotion to the Holy Name of Jesus. He died during a preaching tour at Aquila, where he was buried.

21 May
Saint Christopher Magallanes, Priest, and Companions, Martyrs
Optional Memorial

The Feast recalls the martyrdom of twenty-two priests and three laymen in Mexico between 1915 and 1937. These witnesses include St Christopher Magallanes (Cristóbal Magellanes Jara, 1869-1927) who as a priest founded a seminary in his hometown of Totatiche and ministered zealously in the face of persecution. He was heard to shout from his cell: "I am innocent and I die innocent. I forgive with all my heart those responsible for my death, and I ask God that the shedding of my blood serve the peace of our divided Mexico".

22 May
Saint Rita of Cascia, Religious
Optional Memorial

St Rita of Cascia (1381-1457) was born near Spoleto and, despite wanting to enter the religious life, spent nearly twenty years in a difficult marriage. After the deaths of her husband and two sons, she joined the Augustinian house at Cascia in Umbria. She is known as the 'saint of the impossible.'

In Australia

24 May

Our Lady, Help of Christians, Patron of Australia

Solemnity

Our Lady has proved herself to be the help of Christians over the centuries, both individually and collectively. The title 'Help of Christians' is an ancient one and was especially linked by St Pius V to the Christian victory at Lepanto (1571). The Feast was instituted by Pius VII to commemorate his entry into Rome on 24 May 1814, following release from captivity under Napoleon. St John Bosco had a great devotion to Our Lady, Help of Christians, who is also patron of Australia.

25 May

Saint Bede the Venerable, Priest and Doctor of the Church

Optional Memorial (In England: Memorial)

St Bede the Venerable (673-735) is currently the only English-born Doctor of the Church. He was a monk at Jarrow and wrote Biblical commentaries and historical books, most notably the Ecclesiastical History of the English People. He helped introduce the notion of dating from the Incarnation of Christ (A.D.) and is known as the 'Father of Church History.'

Saint Gregory VII, Pope

Optional Memorial

St Gregory VII (c.1021-1085) was born in Tuscany and entered the monastic life. He worked closely with several popes until he himself was elected to the See of Peter in 1073. He courageously fought against simony, clerical immorality, and the abuse of lay investiture. However, his reformist zeal earned for him the enmity of the Emperor Henry IV. He was exiled to Salerno, where he died in 1085.

Saint Mary Magdalene de' Pazzi, Virgin

Optional Memorial

St Mary Magdalene de' Pazzi (1566-1607) belonged to one of the wealthiest families in Florence, but joined the Discalced Carmelites when she was sixteen, living a life of prayer, penance and humility. She was privileged by mystical experiences, exchanging her heart with that of Jesus and reliving the sufferings of the Passion, but she also endured many years of spiritual dryness. She used to say, 'you know, Lord, that my soul has desired nothing apart from you.'

26 May

Saint Philip Neri, Priest

Memorial

St Philip Neri (1515-1595) was born in Florence but spent most of his life in Rome and is known as the city's 'apostle'. He had a mystical experience in the catacombs in 1544, when he 'felt himself divinely filled with the power of the Spirit', causing his heart to dilate. Ordained in 1551, he founded the Congregation of the Oratory. He was noted for his constant joy and the love he showed those who came to him for counsel or confession.

27 May

Saint Augustine of Canterbury, Bishop

Optional Memorial (In England: Feast)

St Augustine of Canterbury (+ c.604) was a monk at St Andrew's on the Celian Hill in Rome. He was sent by Pope

St Gregory the Great to convert the English people. Landing in Thanet, Kent in 597, he baptised King Ethelbert and many of his subjects. He founded a monastery and a cathedral at Canterbury, and established sees at Rochester and London.

31 May

The Visitation of the Blessed Virgin Mary

Feast

The Visitation commemorates the meeting between Mary and her cousin St Elizabeth at Ein Kerem, just outside Jerusalem. Feeling the presence of his Divine Saviour, St John the Baptist leapt in his mother's womb on the Blessed Virgin's arrival. Following St Elizabeth's words of greeting, Our Lady proclaimed the Magnificat, a hymn praising the Lord for all that He had done for His handmaid and expressing her attitude of faith and humility.

Saturday following the Second Sunday after Pentecost

The Immaculate Heart of the Blessed Virgin Mary

Memorial

Devotion to the Immaculate Heart of Mary originated with St John Eudes in the seventeenth century and developed in parallel to devotion to the Sacred Heart of Jesus. Whereas the Sacred Heart shows the infinite love of God for mankind, Mary's Immaculate Heart presents us with a model for how we should love God. Honouring her Immaculate Heart not only rightly acknowledges her unique privileges but also leads us to her Son.

JUNE

1 June
Saint Justin, Martyr
Memorial

St Justin (+ c.165) was born in Nablus, Samaria and, having studied Platonist philosophy, converted to Christianity at the age of about thirty-three. As a lay apologist he travelled around preaching the faith, defending it from attack and writing works such as the Apologies and Dialogue. He was beheaded in Rome during the reign of Marcus Aurelius.

2 June
Saints Marcellinus and Peter, Martyrs
Optional Memorial

SS Marcellinus and Peter (+ c.304) were members of the Church of Rome; St Marcellinus was a zealous priest and St Peter an exorcist (one of the minor orders). They were beheaded under Diocletian. One tradition says their executioner subsequently became a Christian and related the story of their martyrdom to Pope St Damasus. Their names are included in the Roman Canon.

3 June
Saint Charles Lwanga and Companions, Martyrs
Memorial

The Ugandan martyrs suffered under King Mwanga of the Baganda in 1885-1886. They included St Joseph Mkasa, master of the pages at court, who had criticised Mwanga and was beheaded on 15 November 1885, and his successor St Charles Lwanga, who was burned alive with other Christians (of several denominations) on 3 June 1886 at Namugongo. The martyrs were canonised in 1964 by Paul VI, who visited the shrine at Namugongo five years later.

In Ireland

Saint Kevin, Abbot

Memorial

St Kevin (+ c.618) founded the abbey of Glendalough, County Wicklow. Further information about his life is found only in much later documents; these say he was born into a family of Leinster nobility, was baptised by St Cronan and educated at the monastery of Kilmanach, near Dublin. After living as a hermit for seven years, he founded a monastery. He may have made a pilgrimage to Rome and died, it is said, at the age of 120.

5 June

Saint Boniface, Bishop and Martyr

Memorial

St Boniface (c.673-c.754) was born at Crediton in Devon (England). As a child he entered a Benedictine community and in 716 set out for his first missionary expedition to Frisia. This was unsuccessful but he returned two years later, with papal approval, and evangelised much of southern Germany. He was eventually named Archbishop of Mainz. In his seventies he embarked on a new missionary enterprise in Holland but was martyred at Dokkum in Frisia and buried at the monastery he had founded in Fulda (Germany).

6 June

Saint Norbert, Bishop

Optional Memorial

St Norbert (1080-1134) was born in Xanten (Germany) and lived a worldly life at court until the age of thirty-five, when he experienced a conversion of heart following an accident. He was ordained a priest and established the Canons Regular of Prémontré (Norbertines). In 1126 he was appointed Archbishop of Magdeburg and, despite meeting much opposition, reformed the clergy, defended orthodoxy and promoted the unity and liberty of the Church.

In Ireland

Saint Jarlath, Bishop

Optional Memorial

St Jarlath (+ c.550) is an obscure saint. He may have been born in Galway, and is said to have founded a monastery at Cluain Fois, near Tuam. His pupils may have included St Brendan of Clonfert and St Colman of Munster and he is venerated as first Bishop of Tuam.

In Ireland

7 June

Saint Colman, Bishop

Optional Memorial

St Colman of Dromore (sixth century) was born either in Ulster or Argyll, allegedly of the royal family of Cashel. Reputedly educated at the monastic school of Nendrum on Mahee Island, he went on to become first abbot and bishop of Dromore, County Down.

9 June

Saint Ephrem, Deacon and Doctor of the Church

Optional Memorial

St Ephrem (c.306-373) was born in Nisibis, Mesopotamia, and became a monk and deacon near Edessa (now in Turkey). He wrote Scriptural commentaries, hymns and poems through which he combatted Arianism and encouraged devotion, especially to Our Lady. He has been called 'the Harp of the Holy Ghost' and was declared a Doctor of the Church in 1920.

In England, Ireland and Scotland

Saint Columba (Colum Cille), Abbot and Missionary
Secondary Patron of Ireland

In Ireland and Scotland: Feast; In England: Optional Memorial

St Columba or Columcille (c.521-597), one of the 'Twelve Apostles of Ireland,' was born in Gartan, County Donegal. He founded monasteries at Derry, Durrow and Kells but felt compelled to leave Ireland as an act of penance around 563. With twelve companions he settled on Iona, just off the Isle of Mull, and this became the effective base for the evangelization of Scotland and northern England. He died in 597 and his relics were later translated to Dunkeld.

---

11 June

Saint Barnabas, Apostle

Memorial

St Barnabas (first century) is frequently mentioned in the Acts of the Apostles. He introduced St Paul to the Twelve and accompanied him on his first missionary journey. St Barnabas was present at the Council of Jerusalem and has long been honoured as an Apostle, although he was not one of the Twelve. Different traditions assert that he was martyred in his native Cyprus, or at Salamis in Greece; he has also, improbably, been claimed as the first Bishop of Milan. His name is included in the Roman Canon.

13 June

Saint Anthony of Padua,
Priest and Doctor of the Church

Memorial

St Anthony of Padua (1195-1231) was born in Lisbon (Portugal) and joined the Canons Regular of St Augustine and then the Franciscans at Coimbra. He became famous as a learned theologian, eloquent preacher and worker of miracles – he is still popularly invoked for finding lost objects. He is known as the 'Evangelical Doctor' and was canonised the year after his death.

In Ireland

14 June

Saint Davnet, Virgin

Optional Memorial

St Davnet or Damnat (sixth century) was a nun at Sliabh Beagh, County Monaghan. She is sometimes identified with St Dymphna, the popular virgin martyr who fled overseas and was decapitated by her own father at Gheel (Belgium); Dymphna is invoked as patron of the mentally ill.

In England

16 June

Saint Richard of Chichester, Bishop

Optional Memorial

St Richard of Chichester (1197-1253) was born at Droitwich and educated at Oxford, Paris and Bologna. For a period he was Chancellor of Oxford University and legal adviser to the Archbishop of Canterbury, before being appointed bishop of Chichester in 1244. He lived simply and was generous to the poor. He died at Dover while preaching the crusade.

19 June

Saint Romuald, Abbot

Optional Memorial

St Romuald (c.950-1027) was born at Ravenna (Italy) of a noble family and joined the Cluniac monastery of San Miniato. He founded houses at Fonte Avellana and Camaldoli, which became the mother house of an Order of hermit monks following the Rule of St Benedict. He died in 1027 after a life of prayer and rigorous penance.

In Ireland

20 June

The Irish Martyrs

Memorial

In 1992 Blessed John Paul II beatified seventeen representative martyrs who suffered in Ireland during the sixteenth and seventeenth centuries. They include bishops, priests and lay men and women, such as Blessed Margaret Ball, a wife and mother who helped shelter priests and died in prison in 1584, and the Wexford martyrs (a baker and three sailors) who suffered in 1581.

In England
Saint Alban, Martyr
Optional Memorial

St Alban (+ c.209, or c.254) was a citizen of Verulamium (now St Albans, Hertfordshire) who converted to Christianity, it is said after sheltering a fugitive priest. He was beheaded on Holmhurst Hill, where an abbey was later built. St Alban is the Protomartyr of England.

In Wales
Saints Alban, Julius and Aaron, Protomartyrs of Britain
Optional Memorial

For St Alban see above.

SS Julius and Aaron (+ c.305) suffered at Caerleon-upon-Usk, possibly under Diocletian.

These martyrs are a witness to the early existence of the faith in England and Wales.

---

21 June

Saint Aloysius Gonzaga, Religious
Memorial

St Aloysius Gonzaga (1568-1591) belonged to one of the great Italian noble families and served as a page at several princely courts. At the age of eighteen he embraced a life of poverty and obedience by joining the Society of Jesus. He showed great piety and died as a result of his heroic nursing of the plague-stricken in 1591. He has been declared protector of students and patron of Christian youth.

22 June

Saint Paulinus of Nola, Bishop

Optional Memorial (In Australia: 23 June)

St Paulinus (335-431) was born of a patrician Roman family at Bordeaux (France). While still a pagan he held several public offices and married. However, after his baptism and the death of his only child, he retired to Spain with his wife, Therasia, where they followed a life of prayer, study and penance. He moved to Nola, in Campania, and became bishop in 409. He showed much courage during the invasion of the Goths and is remembered for his poems and letters.

Saints John Fisher, Bishop, and Thomas More, Martyrs

Optional Memorial (In England: Feast; In Australia: Memorial)

St John Fisher (1469-1535) was born at Beverley (Yorkshire) and studied at the University of Cambridge, which he eventually served as Chancellor. In 1504 he became Bishop of Rochester and proved to be a model bishop; indeed, St Charles Borromeo hung his portrait in his apartment with that of St Ambrose. Imprisoned after refusing to take the Oath of Supremacy, Pope Paul III created him a Cardinal. He was beheaded on Tower Hill, London on 22 June 1535.

St Thomas More (1477-1535) was born in London (England). He was a well-respected lawyer and humanist scholar and served as Chancellor to King Henry VIII. He was devoted to his family and managed to maintain his life of prayer amid his many duties. St Thomas retired from public life as the King attempted to annul his marriage to Catherine of Aragon. He was eventually beheaded on Tower Hill on 6 July 1535. Blessed John Paul II declared him patron of politicians in 2000.

In Australia: Optional Memorial

23 June

Saint Paulinus of Nola, Bishop

See 22 June.

In England

23 June

Saint Etheldreda (Audrey), Virgin

Optional Memorial

St Etheldreda (Gthelthryth) or Audrey (c.630-679) is one of the most popular royal saints of the Saxon period. She was the daughter of the powerful King Anna of East Anglia and married twice, the second time to King Egfrith of Northumberland. St Etheldreda eventually took the veil and founded a double monastery on the Isle of Ely. She died on 23 June 679.

---

24 June

The Nativity of Saint John the Baptist

Solemnity

Born six months before Our Lord, St John the Baptist was the son of St Zechariah and St Elizabeth. He was the last and greatest of the prophets and, as the forerunner of the Saviour, he prepared for the coming of Christ. The celebration of his earthly birthday marks the coming of the new dispensation.

27 June

Saint Cyril of Alexandria, Bishop and Doctor of the Church

Optional Memorial

St Cyril (c.376-444) was born at Alexandria and succeeded his uncle as Patriarch in 412. He battled heresy and took a leading role at the Council of Ephesus in 431, which condemned the teaching of Nestorius. He was declared a Doctor of the Church in 1882.

28 June

Saint Irenaeus, Bishop and Martyr

Memorial

St Irenaeus (c.130-c.200) was a disciple of St Polycarp, who was himself a disciple of St John the Evangelist. His writings safeguarded the unity of belief in the face of the Gnostic heretics. He became bishop of Lyons and is venerated as a martyr.

29 June

Saints Peter and Paul, Apostles

Solemnity

St Peter (+ c.64) was the brother of St Andrew and a Galilean fisherman. He was called by the Lord and, despite his obvious human weaknesses, eventually chosen as the leader of the Twelve, the 'rock' on which the Church was built. After Pentecost, he became particularly associated with Antioch and then Rome. He was crucified under Nero and buried at the Vatican.

St Paul (+ c.64/67) was a tent-maker from Tarsus (then capital of the Roman province of Cilicia, now in Turkey), a Pharisee and a Roman citizen. He was initially a persecutor of Christians but was converted by the Lord on his way to Damascus. He became the Apostle of the Gentiles, preaching the Gospel to the uncircumcised, reaching Greece, Italy, Malta and possibly even Spain. He was beheaded along the Via Ostiense and buried nearby, on the site where the basilica bearing his name now stands.

30 June

The First Martyrs of Holy Roman Church

Optional Memorial

The Church celebrates this feast in memory of the martyrs who suffered during the persecution of Nero, following the fire that destroyed much of Rome in 64 AD. Christians from every background were put to death with ingenious cruelty. This was the same persecution in which Saints Peter and Paul were killed. The blood of the martyrs was indeed the seed of the Church.

JULY

1 July

Saint Oliver Plunket, Bishop and Martyr

Memorial

St Oliver Plunket (1629-1681) was born in Loughcrew, County Meath and related to several aristocratic families. After studying at the Irish College, Rome, he was ordained priest in 1654 and stayed in Rome as a professor and a representative of the Irish bishops. In 1669 he was appointed Archbishop of Armagh and Primate of All Ireland. He did much to reorganise and strengthen the Irish Church, despite being forced into hiding for much of his episcopate. Arrested in 1679 at the time of the Popish Plot, he was hanged, drawn and quartered in London on 1 July 1681: the last Catholic martyr to suffer in England. His body is enshrined in Downside Abbey (Somerset), while his head is at St Peter's, Drogheda.

3 July

Saint Thomas, Apostle

Feast

St Thomas (first century), called 'the twin', is chiefly remembered for doubting the reality of the resurrection until he saw the Lord for himself. Once he was satisfied, he made a heartfelt profession of faith: 'My Lord and my God.' St Thomas, who probably suffered martyrdom as a result of preaching the Gospel in India, comforts us when our faith is weak, encourages us to persevere and demonstrates that 'every doubt can lead to an outcome brighter than any uncertainty' (Benedict XVI).

4 July
Saint Elizabeth of Portugal
Optional Memorial

St Elizabeth of Portugal (1271-1336) was the daughter of King
Peter III of Aragon and was named after her great-aunt, St
Elizabeth of Hungary. She endured an unhappy marriage with
the King of Portugal but performed many works of charity
and peacekeeping. As a widow she lived near the Poor Clare
convent at Coimbra.

5 July
Saint Anthony Zaccaria, Priest
Optional Memorial

St Anthony Mary Zaccaria (1502-1539) was born in Cremona
(Italy) and founded the Clerks Regular of St Paul (Barnabites)
in 1530, one of the new congregations that pushed forward
the reforms of the Catholic Reformation. St Anthony died
at the young age of thirty-six as a result of his unceasing
apostolic labours.

6 July
Saint Maria Goretti, Virgin and Martyr
Optional Memorial

St Maria Goretti (1890-1902) was born in Corinaldo near
Ancona (Italy), the third of six children, and became known
for her cheerfulness and piety. When she was twelve, she was
a victim of an attempted rape and was mortally wounded as
she defended her virginity. She forgave her murderer shortly
before she died in hospital. The culprit was imprisoned and
experienced a conversion of heart; he was present at St Maria's
canonization in 1950 and ended his days as a Capuchin brother.

In Ireland

Saint Moninne, Virgin

Optional Memorial

St Moninne or Monenna (c.435-c.518) is said to have been both baptised and veiled by St Patrick. A friend of St Brigid, she established a community at Sliabh Gullion, County Armagh and retired to Killeevy in her final years, where she was buried; pilgrims still visit her well.

In Australia: Optional Memorial

7 July

Blessed Peter To Rot, Martyr

Blessed Peter To Rot (1912-45) was born in Rakunai, New Britain (Papua New Guinea). His parents belonged to the region's first generation of Catholics. He trained as a catechist and married in 1936, bringing into the world three children. After the Japanese occupation of 1942 and the imprisonment of the local clergy, Blessed Peter worked zealously as the leader of the Catholic community. He was arrested in 1945 and killed shortly afterwards, without trial. He was beatified by Blessed John Paul II in 1995.

In Ireland

Saint Maelruain, Bishop and Abbot

Optional Memorial

St Maelruain (+ 792) was the founding abbot and bishop of the monastery at Tallaght, County Dublin. A gifted teacher, his pupils included St Aengus (Oengus).

In Ireland

8 July

Saint Kilian, Bishop and Martyr

Optional Memorial

St Kilian (+ c.689) may have originated in Mullagh, County Cavan, where there is a church dedicated to him. He was possibly already a bishop when he travelled overseas with eleven disciples, settling eventually at Würzburg (Germany). St Kilian received papal approval for his missionary work in Franconia but was murdered, together with his companions St Colman and St Totnan, after challenging the personal morals of the local ruler, Gozbert.

9 July

Saint Augustine Zhao Rong, Priest, and Companions, Martyrs

Optional Memorial

This Feast commemorates 120 Chinese Martyrs, who suffered between 1648 and 1930. They include European missionaries, such as St Gregory Grassi (1823-1900), the Italian-born Bishop of North Shanxi martyred during the Boxer Rebellion, and indigenous Christians, such as St Augustine Zhao Rong, a diocesan priest put to death in 1815. They were canonised by Blessed John Paul II in 2000.

In Scotland

Our Lady of Aberdeen

Feast

The venerable statue of Our Lady of Aberdeen was saved from destruction during the Reformation and taken to safety in Brussels (Belgium). According to tradition, it was thrown into the river Dee but rescued by Catholics on a ship bound for Ostend and taken to Brussels, where it became known as Our Lady of Good Success. It remains in the church of Notre-Dame-du-Finistère but copies can be found in Scotland, including one in St Mary's Cathedral, Aberdeen.

11 July
Saint Benedict, Abbot, Patron of Europe
Memorial (In Europe: Feast)

St Benedict (c.480-c.547) was born in Norcia (Italy) and was educated in Rome. Turning his back on the worldliness he encountered there, he retired to live as a hermit in a cave near Subiaco. His fame spread and disciples began to join him, whom he organised into twelve small monasteries. He eventually moved to Montecassino, where he founded the famous abbey, and produced his Rule, drawing on the monastic wisdom of the Christian East as well as earlier Western Rules (notably the Regula Magistri) and his own practical experience. He was proclaimed patron of Europe by Pope Paul VI because of his essential influence in the formation of Christendom.

In Wales

12 July
Saint John Jones, Priest and Martyr
Optional Memorial

St John Jones (1559-1598) was born at Clynnog Fawr in Gwynedd (Wales) and joined the Observant Franciscans at Pontoise (France), making his final profession in Rome in 1591. He worked secretly around England until his arrest in 1597. The following year, on 12 July, he was hanged, drawn and quartered outside St Thomas Waterings on the Old Kent Road, London.

13 July

Saint Henry

Optional Memorial

St Henry II (972-1024) succeeded his father, Henry the Quarrelsome, as Duke of Bavaria in 995. In 1002 he was elected Holy Roman Emperor and is remembered as a just ruler, a defender of the Church, a friend of the poor and a model of virtue. He considered becoming a monk after the death of his wife, St Cunegund, but was persuaded to persevere in his imperial vocation. He died on 13 July 1024 and was buried in Bamberg Cathedral, a see which he had founded. St Henry is the patron of Benedictine Oblates.

14 July

Saint Camillus de Lellis, Priest

Optional Memorial

St Camillus de Lellis (1550-1614) was born in Bucchianico (Italy), and spent his youth as a soldier of fortune. Left penniless through gambling, he eventually found employment at a hospital for incurables in Rome. Influenced by St Philip Neri and others, he was ordained a priest by Thomas Goldwell, the last of the old English Catholic bishops. In 1584 St Camillus founded the Servants of the Sick (Camillians), who wore a red cross on their chests and vowed to serve the sick, even at the risk of their lives.

15 July

Saint Bonaventure, Bishop and Doctor of the Church

Memorial

St Bonaventure (1221-1274) was born at Bagnorea (Bagnoregio), near Viterbo (Italy) and entered the Franciscan Order. A friend of St Thomas Aquinas, he taught at the University of Paris

and became Minister General of the Franciscan Order. He
was chosen Archbishop of York (England) in 1265 but never
consecrated. He was eventually created Cardinal Bishop of
Albano and died during the Council of Lyons. Remembered
chiefly for his philosophical and theological works, he is
known as the 'Seraphic Doctor.'

16 July
Our Lady of Mount Carmel
Optional Memorial

This feast honours the Blessed Virgin as patroness of the
Carmelite Order. It later came to be associated with a supposed
vision of St Simon Stock, said to have taken place on 16 July
1251. Wearing the 'Brown Scapular', a symbol of the Carmelite
habit, is a sign of trust in Mary's maternal help, especially at
the hour of death.

20 July
Saint Apollinaris, Bishop and Martyr
Optional Memorial

St Apollinaris (first or second century) may have been a native
of Antioch. He eventually became first bishop of Ravenna
(Italy). He was tortured and martyred for the faith and his cult
became popular in many places.

21 July
Saint Lawrence of Brindisi,
Priest and Doctor of the Church
Optional Memorial

St Lawrence (1559-1619) was born at Brindisi (Italy) and joined
the Capuchins in Verona. A talented theologian and gifted

linguist, he travelled around Europe and became particularly associated with missions to the Jews and Protestants. In 1601 he led the Imperial Army during the capture of Székesfehérvár (Hungary) from the Turks, holding only a crucifix. Having served as Minister General of the Capuchins, he died in Lisbon on 22 July 1619, his sixtieth birthday. Blessed John XXIII declared him a Doctor of the Church in 1959.

22 July
Saint Mary Magdalene
Memorial

St Mary Magdalene (first century), originally from Magdala in Galilee, was one of the Lord's most intimate disciples and is often associated with the woman from whom he drove out seven demons. She remained with the Lord during his last agony on the cross and, according to St Mark and St John, was the first to see him after the resurrection. Tradition relates that she spent her last years as a hermit in Provence (France).

23 July
Saint Bridget, Religious, Patron of Europe
Optional Memorial (In Europe: Feast)

St Bridget (Birgitta) (1303-1373) was born in Sweden and married Ulf Gudmarsson in 1316. It was a happy marriage and the devout couple brought up eight children, including St Catherine of Sweden. After Ulf's death in 1344, she founded a religious community (Bridgettines) and received a number of mystical revelations. She corresponded with European monarchs, promoting peace and the return of the papacy from Avignon to Rome. She made pilgrimages to Jerusalem and Rome, where she spent her final years.

In Wales

Saints Philip Evans and John Lloyd, Priests and Martyrs

Optional Memorial

St Philip Evans (1645-1679) was born in Monmouth, studied at St Omer and entered the Jesuits. Following his ordination in 1675, he worked secretly in Wales until he was arrested as a result of the fictitious 'Popish Plot.' He was hanged, drawn and quartered on 22 July 1679 in Gallows Field (now Richmond Road), Cardiff, professing 'to die for God and religion's sake.'

St John Lloyd (c.1630-1679) was originally from Brecon, studied at Valladolid and worked as a mission priest in Wales for over twenty years. Arrested in 1678, he suffered with St Philip Evans at Cardiff.

24 July

Saint Sharbel Makhlūf, Priest

Optional Memorial

St Sharbel or Charbel (1828-1898) was born in Bekaa-Kafra (Lebanon) and became a Catholic Maronite monk, taking his vows at the monastery of St Maron, Annaya. From 1875 he lived as a hermit, with the Holy Eucharist as the source and summit of his life, and his reputation for holiness spread far and wide. He died on 24 December 1898, having suffered a stroke while celebrating Mass.

In Ireland
Saint Declan, Bishop
Optional Memorial

St Declan (fifth century) is one of the Irish saints whose work of evangelization pre-dated that of St Patrick. He was probably trained on the continent and some writers claim he was consecrated a bishop in Rome. He made Ardmore in County Waterford his principal base and spent his last years as a hermit.

25 July
Saint James, Apostle
Feast

St James (+ 44), the son of Zebedee, was called by the Lord together with his brother St John. He was one of the three apostles, along with St Peter and St John, who witnessed the Transfiguration (Mt 17:1) and the agony in the Garden (Mt 16:37). He was condemned to death by Herod Agrippa and beheaded in the year 44, the first of the Twelve to be martyred. His reputed shrine at Santiago de Compostela (Spain) remains a popular pilgrimage centre.

26 July
Saints Joachim and Anne,
Parents of the Blessed Virgin Mary
Memorial

SS Joachim and Anne were the parents of the Blessed Virgin Mary and the grandparents of the Lord. They remind us that the Word truly became flesh in a particular family. Our devotion to them is an extension of our love of Mary and her Divine Son.

29 July
Saint Martha
Memorial

St Martha (first century) was the sister of Mary and Lazarus. Her house at Bethany was often visited by the Lord, who encouraged her to unite her busy life of work with a life of contemplation. According to tradition, St Martha was eventually driven out of Palestine and settled in Provence (France).

30 July
Saint Peter Chrysologus, Bishop and Doctor of the Church
Optional Memorial

St Peter Chrysologus (c.380-c.450) was born in Imola (Italy) and appointed Bishop of Ravenna in 433. He remained close to the imperial family, with whom he is depicted in a mosaic at Ravenna, and was called 'Chrysologus' or 'Golden Worded' by the Empress Galla Placidia. He is best remembered for his eloquent homilies as well as his battles against heresy. He was declared a Doctor of the Church in 1729.

31 July
Saint Ignatius of Loyola, Priest
Memorial

St Ignatius (1491-1556) was born into a noble family at Loyola (Spain). He was injured at the battle of Pamplona (1521) and experienced a conversion during his convalescence. He went on to write the Spiritual Exercises, study theology at Paris and, with his companions, found the Society of Jesus. The Jesuits have had a huge impact on the reform of the Church, the education of the young and the preaching of the Gospel to every corner of the world.

AUGUST

1 August

Saint Alphonsus Liguori,
Bishop and Doctor of the Church

Memorial

St Alphonsus Liguori (1696-1787) was born in Naples (Italy) and became a priest after training as a lawyer. He founded the Congregation of the Most Holy Redeemer (Redemptorists), which specialised in preaching missions, and in 1762 was appointed Bishop of Sant' Agata dei Goti. He faced much physical suffering and divisions within his Order. His numerous writings, especially on moral theology, earned him the title of Doctor of the Church.

2 August

Saint Eusebius of Vercelli, Bishop

Optional Memorial

St Eusebius (+ 371) was born in Sardinia and brought up in Rome. Around 340 he was named bishop of Vercelli in Piedmont and spent much of his episcopate fighting the Arian heresy, which caused him to be exiled for six years. He is thought to have been the first bishop to live together with many of his clergy in community, and is honoured as co-founder of the Augustinian Canons.

Saint Peter Julian Eymard, Priest

Optional Memorial

St Peter Julian Eymard (1811-1868) was born at La Mure, Isère (France) and joined the Marist Fathers. He dedicated his life to promoting Eucharistic devotion and founded both the Congregation of the Blessed Sacrament and the Servants of the Blessed Sacrament. Canonised in 1962, he is known as the 'Apostle of the Eucharist.'

In Wales

3 August

Saint Germanus of Auxerre, Bishop

Optional Memorial

St Germanus (c.378-448) was Bishop of Auxerre (France). He had close associations with the British Church and visited in 429 and 447 to assist in the fight against the Pelagian heresy. During one of his visits he helped the Britons defeat the Picts and Saxons in battle; since it was around Easter this was known as the 'Alleluia Victory'. As a thanksgiving he made a pilgrimage to the shrine of St Alban. He is traditionally remembered as a monastic founder in Wales.

---

4 August

Saint John Vianney, Priest

Memorial

St John Mary (Jean-Baptiste-Marie) Vianney (1786-1859) was born at Dardilly, near Lyons (France) and, despite finding his seminary studies difficult, was ordained a priest and spent forty-two years as Curé (parish priest) of Ars. Despite encountering much opposition, he reformed the parish, spent hours in the confessional and centred his life on the Holy Eucharist. Pius XI declared him patron of parish clergy.

5 August

The Dedication of the Basilica of Saint Mary Major

Optional Memorial

In 431 the Council of Ephesus declared the Blessed Virgin to be the 'Mother of God' (Theotokos) and shortly afterwards Pope Sixtus III dedicated the restored Basilica of St Mary Major in Rome in her honour. According to tradition its location had originally been indicated by a miraculous shower of snow on 5 August, in the middle of the Roman summer, hence the title 'Our Lady of the Snows'. The basilica is considered the most important church dedicated to the Blessed Virgin Mary and the festival of its dedication renews our links with Rome.

6 August

The Transfiguration of the Lord

Feast

The Transfiguration of the Lord on Mount Tabor came to strengthen the faith of the disciples, for trying times lay ahead: the Son of Man would be put to death and all that the human eye could see was weakness, humiliation and suffering. Beyond the shame of the cross, however, is the light and glory of Easter, and it is this that the Transfiguration reveals. It shows the disciples, and us, Christ's divinity – he who is Light from Light - and anticipates the glory of Heaven.

7 August

Saint Sixtus II, Pope, and Companions, Martyrs

Optional Memorial

St Sixtus (Xystus) II and his companions (+ 258) suffered during the persecution of the Emperor Valerian. Indeed, St Sixtus had to be consecrated Bishop of Rome in secret the previous year and was captured while celebrating the Eucharist. He was beheaded almost immediately in the Cemetery of Praetextatus. According to tradition, six of his seven deacons were also killed on the same day, the seventh (St Lawrence) being martyred a few days later. St Sixtus is included in the Roman Canon.

Saint Cajetan, Priest

Optional Memorial

St Cajetan or Gaetano (1480-1547) was born in Vicenza (Italy) and gave up a promising legal career in order to be ordained a priest in 1516. He co-founded the Congregation of Clerks Regular (Theatines), which did much to promote the reform of the clergy, and he had such zeal in seeking people's salvation that he was called the 'Hunter of Souls.'

In Australia: Optional Memorial

Saint Dominic, Priest

See 8 August

---

8 August
Saint Dominic, Priest

Memorial (In Australia: 7 August)

St Dominic (c.1170-1221) was born at Caleruega (Spain) and initially joined the Canons Regular of Osma. In 1206 he was sent to Languedoc (France) to help uproot the Catharist or Albigensian heresy. While based in Toulouse, he founded the Order of Preachers (Dominicans) to assist in this work; the Order was approved by the Holy See in 1216 and has had a huge impact on the life of the Church.

In Australia

Saint Mary of the Cross, Virgin

Solemnity

St Mary of the Cross (1842-1909) was born Mary MacKillop in Fitzroy, Victoria (Australia) to Scottish parents. While working as a governess she came under the influence of Fr Julian Tenison Woods, who encouraged her to found the Sisters of St Joseph of the Sacred Heart (Josephites), dedicated to the education of poor children. She was canonized on 17 October 2010, the first Australian to be so honoured.

9 August

Saint Teresa Benedicta of the Cross, Virgin and Martyr, Patron of Europe

Optional Memorial (In Europe: Feast)

St Teresa Benedicta (1891-1942) was born Edith Stein at Wrocław (now in Poland, but then in the German province of Silesia), the eleventh child of a Jewish family. She showed great ability in her philosophical studies and became a popular lecturer and writer. After reading the autobiography of St Teresa of Avila, she sought baptism in 1922 and eleven years later joined the Carmelites at Cologne. She was moved to the Carmel of Echt (Netherlands) to avoid the growing Nazi threat but was eventually arrested, and gassed at Auschwitz on 9 August 1942.

In Ireland

Saint Nathy, Bishop

Optional Memorial

St Nathy or Nath N (sixth century) is said to have been a native of Luighne, Sligo and was known as Cruimthir, 'the Priest'.

Much later accounts of his life make him a bishop and founder of a monastery at Achonry, of which diocese he is the patron. He may have been a disciple of St Finnian of Clonard.

In Ireland

Saint Felim, Bishop

Optional Memorial

St Felim (Phelim) or Fedlimid (sixth century) is traditionally thought to have been the son of Dediva, seven of whose children are venerated as saints. He is venerated as the first bishop of Kilmore and the patron of that diocese.

10 August

Saint Lawrence, Deacon and Martyr

Feast

St Lawrence (+ 258) was one of the seven deacons of St Sixtus II killed during the persecution of Valerian. On his arrest, he was ordered to hand over the riches of the Church but pointed to a crowd of poor people, saying 'Here are the true treasures of the Church.' According to tradition, he was roasted to death on a gridiron.

11 August

Saint Clare, Virgin

Memorial

St Clare (c.1193-1253) was born in Assisi (Italy) and became a disciple of St Francis. She founded the Order of the Poor Clares or Minoresses and lived a life of radical poverty at the convent of San Damiano. She wisely led her community for forty years and gave counsel to many high-ranking prelates. Such was the fame of her holiness, she was canonised two years after her death.

12 August
Saint Jane Frances de Chantal, Religious
Optional Memorial

St Jane Frances de Chantal (1572-1641) was born in Dijon (France). She was happily married and had four children. Her husband was killed in a hunting accident; nine years later, with the help of her spiritual director, St Francis de Sales, she founded the Order of the Visitation, which was dedicated to works of charity among the sick and poor.

In Ireland
Saint Muredach, Bishop
Optional Memorial

St Muredach or Murtagh (fifth or more probably sixth century) is sometimes called a disciple of St Patrick, although he is also more probably reckoned a contemporary of St Columba. He is venerated as the first Bishop of Killala and remains the patron of that diocese.

In Ireland
Saint Attracta, Virgin
Optional Memorial

St Attracta or Athracht (fifth or sixth century). Legend says she ran away from home in order to receive the veil from St Patrick at Coolavin. She is said to have founded a number of churches, including a hospice for travellers at Killaraght on Lough Gara.

In Ireland

Saint Lelia, Virgin

Optional Memorial

St Lelia (sixth century) is especially venerated in the diocese of Limerick; almost nothing is known of her life. She probably led a religious community in the province of Munster. She gave her name to Killeely (Cill Liadaini) and is sometimes identified with St Liadhain, whose great-grandfather was baptised by St Patrick at Singland.

13 August

Saints Pontian, Pope, and Hippolytus, Priest, Martyrs

Optional Memorial

SS Pontian and Hippolytus (+ c.236) suffered martyrdom after being exiled to Sardinia by the Emperor Maximinus Thrax. St Pontian succeeded St Urban I as Pope in 230, while St Hippolytus was a priest of Rome. He may also be the noted theologian of that name who was elected anti-pope during a disagreement over the forgiveness of those who had sinned grievously. He was reconciled with the Church before his death.

In Ireland

Saint Fachtna, Bishop

Optional Memorial

St Fachtna or Fachanan (sixth century) was born at Tulachteann and was reputed a disciple of St Ita. He founded monasteries at Molana, near Youghal, and Rosscarbery, County Cork, which later became an important centre of learning. He is patron of the Diocese of Ross.

14 August

Saint Maximilian Mary Kolbe, Priest and Martyr

Memorial

St Maximilian Kolbe (1894-1941) was born near Łodz (Poland) and joined the Conventual Franciscans. Marked by an ardent devotion to the Blessed Virgin, who had appeared to him as a child, he set up the Militia Immaculata, preached Marian consecration and founded monasteries in Niepokalanow (Poland) and Nagasaki (Japan). Eventually imprisoned by the Nazis in Auschwitz, he offered himself in exchange for a father who was to be starved to death. Blessed John Paul II canonised him in 1982 and proclaimed him the patron of the 'suffering' twentieth century.

15 August

The Assumption
of the Blessed Virgin Mary

Solemnity

The Solemnity of the Assumption is, in some ways, the paramount feast of Our Lady, since it commemorates her passing, body and soul, into glory in Heaven, where she stands beside her Son 'in garments of gold'. Though the dogma of the Assumption was only defined in 1950, it was widely believed by the earliest Christians. The Blessed Virgin truly leads the way; she fulfilled her vocation in humility and, given her Immaculate Conception, the grave was no place for her body. Where she is now, we one day hope to be.

16 August
Saint Stephen of Hungary
Optional Memorial

St Stephen (Istvan) (c.975-1038) was baptised at the age of ten, when his father, the Duke of Hungary, converted to Christianity. He married Gisela, sister of the Holy Roman Emperor St Henry, and succeeded his father in 997. Crowned first King of Hungary in 1001, he ruled forcefully and with great wisdom and did much to encourage the evangelisation of his people. His wife was beatified in 1975; his son Emeric (Imre), who predeceased him, is also venerated as a saint.

In Ireland

17 August
Our Lady of Knock
Memorial

In August 1879 fifteen people witnessed an apparition of Our Lady, St Joseph and St John the Evangelist, together with the Lord (as the Lamb of God), outside the church at Knock. It grew into an international shrine and was visited by Blessed John Paul II in 1979.

19 August
Saint John Eudes, Priest
Optional Memorial

St John Eudes (1601-1680) was born in the Norman village of Ri (France), joined the Oratory in Paris and was ordained in 1625. He went on to found the Congregation of Jesus and Mary (Eudists) and the Sisters of Our Lady of Charity of the

Refuge. A popular preacher, he promoted devotion to the Hearts of Jesus and Mary. He was canonised in 1925.

20 August
Saint Bernard, Abbot and Doctor of the Church
Memorial

St Bernard (c.1090-1153) was born into a noble family at Fontaines, near Dijon (France). In 1113 he joined the new monastery at Cîteaux and went on to found the Cistercian house at Clairvaux. St Bernard became known as a talented theologian, preacher and controversialist, enjoying a correspondence with monarchs and popes. He managed to combine a life of action with one of mystical contemplation, as revealed in his writings. Declared a Doctor of the Church in 1830, he is known as 'the last of the Fathers.'

21 August
Saint Pius X, Pope
Memorial

St Pius X (1835-1914) was born in Riese, near Venice (Italy), the son of the village postman. Ordained in 1858, he is one of the few popes to have spent a substantial period in parochial ministry. After serving as Bishop of Mantua and Patriarch of Venice, he succeeded Leo XIII as Pope in 1903. He defended Catholic doctrine against modernism, described as the 'synthesis of all heresies', and also promoted the dignified celebration of the liturgy. Aiming 'to restore all things in Christ', he extended the practice of frequent communion.

22 August

The Queenship of the Blessed Virgin Mary

Memorial

Pope Pius XII instituted this Feast in 1954, to conclude what was then the Octave of the Assumption. We remember that the Blessed Virgin reigns in Heaven, together with her Son; she reigns not because she is equal to God but because she is mother of Christ the King. All her privileges come from her Motherhood of God and the unique role she played in our redemption.

23 August

Saint Rose of Lima, Virgin

Optional Memorial

St Rose (1586-1617) was born in Lima (Peru). Influenced by the example of St Catherine of Siena, she lived a life of prayer and penance and joined the Third Order of St Dominic. The first canonised saint from the Americas, she is venerated as the patron of Latin America and the Philippines.

In Ireland

Saint Eugene, Bishop

Optional Memorial

St Eugene or Eogan (Eoghan) (sixth century) is said to have been sold into slavery as a child and to have spent a period in Brittany. Returning to Ireland, he is said to have joined St Kevin's monastic community at Kilnamanach, County Wicklow, and then helped found the monastery at Clones, County Monaghan. He is venerated as the first bishop of Ardstraw in Tyrone, which later became the See of Derry.

---

24 August
Saint Bartholomew, Apostle
Feast

St Bartholomew (first century) was originally from Cana in Galilee and is usually identified with Nathanael, who was introduced to the Lord by St Philip. According to tradition, after Pentecost he preached the Gospel in Arabia, India and Armenia, where he was flayed alive. He is thus the patron of tanners.

25 August
Saint Louis
Optional Memorial

St Louis IX (1214-1270) became King of France at the age of twelve. He married Margaret of Provence and had eleven children. He showed great integrity in his rule, always promoting peace and justice and showing great piety and love for the poor. He died of dysentery near Tunis in 1270 during his second crusade for the liberation of the Holy Places. He was canonised in 1297.

Saint Joseph Calasanz, Priest
Optional Memorial

St Joseph Calasanz (1557-1648) was born near Peralta de la Sal in Aragon (Spain) and ordained a priest in 1583. He went to Rome, where he joined St Camillus de Lellis in caring for the victims of the 1595 plague. He founded the first free school in the city and his community of teachers developed into the Piarist Order. In his old age he was the victim of false accusations but patiently endured this humiliation. He is the patron of Christian schools.

In England

26 August

Blessed Dominic of the Mother of God, Priest

Optional Memorial

Blessed Dominic Barberi (1792-1849) was born near Viterbo (Italy), entered the Passionists and ordained a priest in 1818. He taught theology in Rome and served as Provincial. He had long believed he was called to be an instrument for the conversion of England and in his final years was given the opportunity of labouring tirelessly in this country, despite facing much opposition. On 8 October 1845 he received Blessed John Henry Newman into the Church at Littlemore.

In Wales

Saint David Lewis, Priest and Martyr

Optional Memorial

St David Lewis (1616-1679) was born in Monmouthshire and brought up as a Protestant. After studying law at the Middle Temple, London, he became a Catholic and studied for the priesthood at the Venerable English College, Rome. After ordination he joined the Jesuits and in 1646 was sent on the English mission, basing himself at the Cwm, Llanrothal on the Welsh border. After thirty-one years of discreet ministry, he was arrested during the hysteria of the 'Popish Plot' and hanged, drawn and quartered at Usk.

27 August
Saint Monica
Memorial

St Monica (c.331-387) was born in Thagaste (now Algeria, then in the Roman provine of Africa). She married Patricius and was mother of St Augustine. She prayed and suffered for her son's conversion and was overjoyed by his baptism in 387. She died shortly afterwards at Ostia and in the fifteenth century her relics were brought to Rome.

28 August
Saint Augustine, Bishop and Doctor of the Church
Memorial

St Augustine (354-430) was born in Thagaste (Algeria) and, despite the example of his mother, became a Manichean and fathered an illegitimate child. He was converted at the age of thirty-three and baptised by St Ambrose in Milan. St Augustine became Bishop of Hippo Regius (now Annaba, Algeria) and wrote and preached energetically in defence of the faith, making him one of the most influential Doctors of the Church. His principles concerning the religious life continue to inspire Augustinian canons, friars and nuns.

29 August
The Passion of Saint John the Baptist
Memorial

The Gospels relate how St John fearlessly condemned Herod Antipas's unlawful marriage to Herodias, who had been previously married to his half-brother. The outraged Herodias had him imprisoned. In a moment of weakness Herod promised to grant the heart's desire of Salome, the daughter of Herodias. She asked for St John's head, which was promptly fetched for her. Thus the Precursor of the Lord preceded his Master through his passion.

In England

30 August

Saints Margaret Clitherow, Anne Line and Margaret Ward, Martyrs

Optional Memorial

This day commemorates the three canonised female martyrs of the English Reformation: St Margaret Clitherow (1556-1586), a native of York and convert to Catholicism, who sheltered priests and was pressed to death in her home town on 25 March 1586; St Anne Line (1567-1601) from Dunmow, Essex who also harboured priests and was hanged at Tyburn on 27 February 1601; St Margaret Ward (+ 1588), born in Congleton, Cheshire, who worked in London and attempted to help a priest escape from prison. She was hanged at Tyburn on 30 August 1588. All three were canonised in 1970 amongst the Forty Martyrs of England and Wales.

In Ireland

Saint Fiacre, Monk

Optional Memorial

St Fiacre (seventh century) was born in Ireland and felt called to live as a hermit. After living in solitude in County Kilkenny, he moved to France and settled at Breuil. Here he cultivated the land, built a chapel and established a hospice for travellers. He was widely venerated in France and his relics were eventually translated to Meaux.

In England

31 August

Saint Aidan, Bishop, and Saints of Lindisfarne

Optional Memorial

St Aidan or Aedan (+ 651) was an Irish monk who joined the community at Iona and was sent to preach the Gospel in Northumbria. He was consecrated bishop and settled on the island of Lindisfarne, with the support of King St Oswald and his successor St Oswin. After St Aidan's death in 651, the 'Holy Island' of Lindisfarne continued to produce many saints instrumental in the evangelisation of northern England, until the monastery was devastated by Vikings. These saints include the bishops St Finan, St Colman, St Eata, St Eadfrith, and, of course, St Cuthbert (4 September).

In Ireland

Saint Aidan of Lindisfarne, Bishop and Missionary

Optional Memorial

See above

SEPTEMBER

3 September

Saint Gregory the Great,
Pope and Doctor of the Church

Memorial (In England: Feast)

St Gregory the Great (540-604) belonged to a Roman patrician family and served as a magistrate before embracing the monastic life. He acted as papal legate at Constantinople and was elected Pope in 590. He tightened Church discipline and liturgical practice, reorganised the lands belonging to the Holy See and sent St Augustine to convert the Kingdom of Kent. He is consequently called the 'Apostle of the English' and, thanks to his theological and pastoral writings, is a Doctor of the Church.

In England

4 September

Saint Cuthbert, Bishop

Optional Memorial

St Cuthbert (c.634-687) worked as a shepherd in Northumbria until he joined the monastic community at Melrose under St Eata. He moved to Lindisfarne and did much to spread the Gospel in the area, before embracing the eremitical life on the isle of Farne. In 684 he became Bishop of Hexham, but quickly exchanged Sees with St Eata, who was by now Bishop of Lindisfarne. He was known for the holiness of his life and his many miracles. Buried originally at Lindisfarne, his body was later translated to Durham and found to be incorrupt.

In Ireland
Saint Mac Nissi, Bishop
Optional Memorial

St Mac Nissi (Macanisius, Oengus Mac Nisse) (+ 514) was possibly baptised by St Patrick. He was a hermit at Kells, and has been associated with the founding of the monastery there. He is claimed as first bishop of Connor in County Antrim.

8 September
The Nativity of the Blessed Virgin Mary
Feast

Nothing is known for sure about the details of the Blessed Virgin's birth. Even her parents, traditionally known as St Joachim and St Anne, are not mentioned in Sacred Scripture. Today's feast originated in the East, probably during the sixth century, and was later introduced to the West. A French legend tells of a man hearing angels singing on the night of 8 September and being told that the Virgin Mary had been born on that night. Her earthly birth is celebrated (like that of St John the Baptist) because it announced to the world the coming of Jesus, the beginning of the New Covenant.

9 September
Saint Peter Claver, Priest
Optional Memorial

St Peter Claver (1580-1654) was born at Verdú in Catalonia (Spain) and entered the Society of Jesus. In 1610 he was sent to Colombia and began his life's work among the slaves. He cared for them and baptised more than 300,000 during his thirty-three years of tireless ministry.

In Ireland

Saint Ciaran, Abbot

Memorial

St Ciaran or Kieran (c.512-c.545), one of the 'Twelve Apostles of Ireland,' was born in Connaught and studied under St Finnian at Clonard. He eventually founded the great monastery of Clonmacnoise on the Shannon, which became an important centre of learning. However, after serving as Abbot for only seven months he died.

In Wales

11 September

Saint Deiniol, Bishop

Optional Memorial

St Deiniol (Daniel) (sixth century). Legend makes him a descendant (perhaps a grandson) of Pabo Post Prydyn ("the Pillar of Britain"), a north British hero who, again according to legend, renounced the world and died a hermit in Anglesey. Deiniol founded the monasteries of Bangor Fawr on the Menai strait and Bangor Iscoed on the Dee. Bangor Cathedral is dedicated to him and he is sometimes reckoned its first bishop. He was buried on Bardsey Island (Ynys Ynlli).

12 September

The Most Holy Name of Mary

Optional Memorial

The name of Mary is regarded as holy because it is the name of the Mother of God, her who brought the Saviour into the world. The Feast of the Most Holy Name of Mary was added to the Universal Calendar in 1684 by Blessed Innocent XI, commemorating the defeat of the Turks at the gates of Vienna the previous year: a powerful example of the might of the Blessed Virgin's intercession.

In Ireland

Saint Ailbe, Bishop

Optional Memorial

St Ailbe or Elvis (sixth century) is another Irish saint of whom little is known but about whom there are many legends. He is said to have been consecrated bishop in Rome, to have preached throughout Ireland, making many converts, and to have written a Rule for monks. He is venerated as founder of the See of Emly.

---

13 September

Saint John Chrysostom, Bishop and Doctor of the Church

Memorial

St John Chrysostom (c.350-407) was born at Antioch and trained as a lawyer. He became a monk, then later a priest and became a famed theologian and preacher, gaining the name Chrysostom or 'the golden-mouthed.' In 398 he became Archbishop of Constantinople and faced much opposition in his reforms. He died in exile and is honoured as one of the four Greek Doctors of the Church. The Divine Liturgy of St John Chrysostom, widely used in the East, was once attributed to him, although it is now recognised as very probably later than his time.

14 September
The Exaltation of the Holy Cross
Feast

The Feast of the Exaltation of the Holy Cross commemorates
the rescue of the relic of the True Cross by Emperor Heraclius
in 629 after it had been captured by the Persians; it also marks
the original dedication of the Church of the Holy Sepulchre,
where relics of the Cross were kept, in 335. The Feast celebrates
the Cross, the instrument of our salvation, and is in many ways
an extension of Good Friday. The Cross is a great and powerful
sign of God's love for us – a love stronger than death – and also
a daily reality in our lives: the only true path to holiness.

15 September
Our Lady of Sorrows
Memorial

This feast originated as a memorial of the Seven Sorrows of
Mary, most of which were linked to the events of Good Friday,
when she stood at the foot of the cross. We remember that the
Blessed Virgin had to live through the personal tragedy of seeing
her Son die. She had a unique share in our redemption, offering
her Son's life to the Lord, trusting that it was part of his plan.

16 September
Saints Cornelius, Pope, and Cyprian, Bishop, Martyrs
Memorial

St Cornelius (+ 253) was elected Pope in succession to St
Fabian and actively fought the errors of Novatian, who denied
that those who had lapsed from the faith could be reconciled.
He died while exiled in Civitavecchia (Italy) and is venerated
as a martyr.

St Cyprian (+ 258) was another leading opponent of Novatianism. He was Bishop of Carthage and one of the earliest victims of the persecution under the Emperor Valerian. Both saints are included in the Roman Canon.

In Scotland

Saint Ninian, Bishop

Feast

St Ninian (+ c.432) is thought to have been a British bishop who was educated in Rome and sent to preach the Gospel to the Picts. He built a 'white house' or stone church at Whithorn, south of Wigtown (Scotland), which was his base and the site of a monastic community. St Ninian is witness to the antiquity of the Church in Scotland and its early links with the Holy See.

---

17 September

Saint Robert Bellarmine, Bishop and Doctor of the Church

Optional Memorial

St Robert Bellarmine (1542-1621) was born at Montepulciano (Italy) and joined the Society of Jesus. He was later created a Cardinal and was briefly Archbishop of Capua, although his greatest legacy is as a theologian and controversialist, especially in defending the Church from its Protestant critics. He was canonised only in 1930, and declared a Doctor of the Church the following year.

19 September

Saint Januarius, Bishop and Martyr

Optional Memorial

St Januarius (+ c.304) was Bishop of Benevento in Italy. He was martyred, possibly by beheading during the persecution of Diocletian, and is venerated as patron of Naples. His dried blood contained in a phial famously liquifies three times a year, including on his feast.

In England

Saint Theodore of Canterbury, Bishop

Optional Memorial

St Theodore (c.602-690) was born in Tarsus (now in Turkey, but then part of the Greek-speaking Eastern Empire) and studied at Antioch and Constantinople; eventually he joined a community of Eastern monks in Rome. He was the surprise choice of Pope St Vitalian as Archbishop of Canterbury, taking possession of the See on 27 May 669. His episcopate proved to be an important one: he presided over a council of the whole English Church at Hertford in 672, established an influential school for clergy at Canterbury (he was a remarkably learned man), intervened in the dispute between St Wilfrid and St Chad, created new dioceses and promoted reform of the Church.

---

20 September

Saints Andrew Kim Tae-gŏn, Priest, and Paul Chŏng Ha-sang, and Companions, Martyrs

Memorial

The Korean Martyrs testify to the presence of the faith in that region from the eighteenth century and the terrible persecutions during the nineteenth century. Outstanding among them were St Andrew Kim Tae-gŏn (1821-1846), the first Korean-born priest who was tortured and beheaded near Seoul in 1846, and St Paul Chŏng Ha-sang (c.1794-1839), a lay catechist who was crucified on 22 September 1839. More than 8,000 Christians from all walks of life lost their lives during the persecution and 103 of them were canonised in 1994.

21 September
Saint Matthew, Apostle and Evangelist
Feast

St Matthew (first century), also called Levi, was the son of Alphaeus. He worked as a tax collector for the Romans, a despised profession, when he was called by the Lord at Capernaum. Nevertheless, Jesus Christ called him to be an Apostle. After the Ascension he may have travelled to Persia or to Ethiopia; wherever it was, he was martyred. St Matthew's Gospel stands first in the New Testament, and his name appears among the other Apostles in the Roman Canon.

23 September
Saint Pius of Pietrelcina, Priest
Memorial

St Pius (1887-1968), better known as Padre Pio, was born in Pietrelcina in Campania (Italy) and joined the Capuchin community at Morcone. Ordained in 1910, he moved six years later to San Giovanni Rotondo in the Gargano peninsula. Bearing the wounds of Christ's passion on his body (known as stigmata), he became famous for his ministry in the confessional, his spiritual direction and his miracles. In 1956 he opened the 'Home to Relieve Suffering' near his friary.

Despite his popularity, he faced much opposition, even from Church authorities. He was canonised in 2002.

In Ireland

Saint Eunan (Adomnan), Abbot

Optional Memorial

St Eunan or Adomnan (c.627-704) was born at Drumhome in County Donegal and was related to St Columba. He joined the monastery at Iona and became its ninth Abbot in 679. He visited Northumbria several times, promoted Roman customs and wrote several works, including the Life of St Columba. He was also responsible for 'Adomnan's Law' which, among other things, protected non-combatants in times of warfare.

In England

24 September

Our Lady of Walsingham

Memorial

England's premier Marian shrine dates back to 1061, when a wealthy widow, Richeldis de Faverches, was inspired by a vision to build a replica of the Holy House of Nazareth in Walsingham, Norfolk. This remained a vibrant pilgrimage centre until its destruction in 1538, although the shrine was later revived by both Catholics (1897) and Anglicans (1922). Formerly, 24 September was kept as the Memorial of Our Lady of Ransom, when prayers were offered for the 'ransom' of England, 'Our Lady's Dowry.'

In Ireland

25 September

Saint Finbarr, Bishop

Optional Memorial

St Finbarr (Finbar, Barry) (c.560-c.610) may have been born at Lisnacaheragh, County Cork. After a period preaching in southern Ireland and living as a hermit on Lough Eiroe, he founded a monastery at Etargabail. His greatest foundation was the monastery at Cork – he is venerated as the city's founder, patron and first bishop. According to legend, when he died the sun did not set for a fortnight.

26 September

Saints Cosmas and Damian, Martyrs

Optional Memorial

St Cosmas and St Damian (date uncertain; perhaps + c.300). According to tradition, they were twins who worked as doctors and were known as the Anargyri ('the silverless') on account of their practice of not charging for their services. They brought many of their patients to Christ but were finally condemned to death under Diocletian around the year 300 and suffered at Cyrrhus (Syria). Their basilica in Rome, not far from the Colosseum, was built in the sixth century by Felix IV and their names appear in the Roman Canon.

27 September
Saint Vincent de Paul, Priest
Memorial

St Vincent de Paul (1581-1660) was born in Gascony (France) and ordained a priest at the early age of twenty. He is said to have endured a period of captivity in Tunis; at any rate, after being falsely accused of theft, he dedicated himself to evangelizing the poor, the unfortunate and the suffering. He founded the Congregation of Priests of the Mission (Lazarists) and, together with St Louise de Marillac, the Daughters of Charity. These congregations, together with the well-known Society of St Vincent de Paul, continue his charitable work today.

28 September
Saint Wenceslaus, Martyr
Optional Memorial

St Wenceslaus (Wenceslas, Vaclav) (907-930) was born in the castle of Stochov near Prague and became Duke of Bohemia in 921. The popular carol 'Good King Wenceslas' speaks of his strong faith and concern for the poor. However, he faced many trials in governing as a Christian prince and was finally murdered at the instigation of his brother, Boleslav, on 27 September 929. According to legend, his final words were, 'Brother, may God forgive you.'

Saint Lawrence Ruiz and Companions, Martyrs
Optional Memorial

These sixteen Dominican martyrs suffered at Nishizaka Hill, near Nagasaki (Japan) in September 1637 during the persecution of the Tokugawa shogunate. Many of them were bound and hanged upside down, causing a slow death. They included St Lawrence (Lorenzo) Ruiz (c.1600-1637), a lay member of the Dominican Confraternity of the Holy Rosary and a father of three, who is the first Filipino saint.

29 September
Saints Michael, Gabriel and Raphael, Archangels
Feast

The Feast celebrates the three archangels named in Sacred Scripture, reminding us of the angelic world and of their constant ministrations to the world.

St Michael (meaning 'Who is like God') is venerated as captain of the heavenly army, victor over Satan, protector of the Church and helper of the sick and dying. Today's feast originated as that of the dedication of a Roman basilica in his honour.

St Gabriel (meaning 'Strength of God') announced both the birth of St John the Baptist (to Zechariah) and of Jesus Christ (to the Blessed Virgin Mary). His greeting at the Annunciation, 'Hail, full of grace,' has become one of the most familiar prayers.

St Raphael (meaning 'God heals') took care of Tobias on his journey, as described in the book of Tobit, and is often associated with the angel of the sheep pool (Jn 5:1-4). He is a patron of the blind, travellers and physicians and nurses.

30 September
Saint Jerome, Priest and Doctor of the Church
Memorial

St Jerome (Hieronymus) (c.342-420) was born in Strido (now in Croatia, then part of the Roman province of Dalmatia) and studied in Rome, where he was baptised. He retired for a while to Syria to live as a hermit and learnt Hebrew at the hands of a rabbi. Between 382 and 385 he was in Rome as secretary to Pope Damasus, who commissioned him to revise the Latin version of the Bible. He went to Bethlehem to concentrate on this work, together with the writing of Scriptural commentaries and theological works.

OCTOBER

1 October

Saint Thérèse of the Child Jesus, Virgin and Doctor of the Church

Memorial

St Thérèse Martin (1873-1897) was born at Alençon and, aged fifteen, entered the Carmel of Lisieux, thus joining two of her sisters. Although she died of tuberculosis at the age of twenty-four, such was the influence of her spiritual writings and her 'little way' that she was declared a Doctor of the Church by Blessed John Paul II in 1997. She is also Patron of the Missions and Co-Protectress of France (with St Joan of Arc).

2 October

The Holy Guardian Angels

Memorial

Three days ago the Church's liturgy celebrated the Archangels SS Michael, Gabriel and Raphael; today is the turn of those angels who, according to Scripture and tradition, guard and assist us at every moment. Each person has such a Guardian Angel and we rightly rejoice in their company.

4 October

Saint Francis of Assisi

Memorial

St Francis (c.1182-1226) was the son of a wealthy merchant in Assisi (Italy) and, responding to the Lord's call, embraced poverty and preached the love of God to all. In 1210 Innocent

III approved his Order of Friars Minor (Franciscans); two years later he helped St Clare establish a female community (Poor Clares). In 1224, while praying at La Verna, he received the wounds of the crucified Lord, which caused him great pain in his final years.

6 October

Saint Bruno, Priest

Optional Memorial

St Bruno (c.1035-1101), founder of the Carthusian Order, was born in Cologne and taught theology for about twenty years at Rheims (France). In 1084 he retired with six companions into the mountains near Grenoble (France) and founded the strict monastery of the Grande Chartreuse. St Bruno was summoned to Rome by his former pupil, Blessed Urban II, and while working for the pope founded further monasteries in Italy.

7 October

Our Lady of the Rosary

Memorial

This Memorial (originally Our Lady of Victories) commemorates the battle of Lepanto (7 October 1571), when a Christian fleet defeated the Turks. The victory was attributed by Pope St Pius V to the recitation of the Holy Rosary. This great Marian prayer is sometimes traced back to St Dominic and his confrères, preaching against the Albigensian heresy in the thirteenth century, although it seems more likely to have taken its familiar form in the fifteenth century. Since then it has spread all over the world and has produced marvellous fruits, bringing countless Christians 'to Jesus through Mary.'

9 October

Saint Denis, Bishop, and Companions, Martyrs

Optional Memorial

St Denis (+ c.258) is venerated as the first bishop of Paris and patron of France. He is said to have been sent to Gaul by Pope Fabian and to have been beheaded at Montmartre with Rusticus, a priest, and Eleutherius, a deacon. Some writers wrongly identified him with Dionysius the Areopagite, mentioned in Acts 17:34, who was claimed as author of a series of works of mystical theology actually written in the fifth century. The great Abbey of Saint Denis in Paris is the resting place of many Kings and Queens of France.

Saint John Leonardi, Priest

Optional Memorial

St John Leonardi (c.1542-1609) was born near Lucca (Italy) and after training as a pharmacist, was ordained a priest. This allowed him to bring to people the 'medicine of God,' Jesus Christ. He founded the Clerks Regular of the Mother of God and also helped establish the College of 'Propaganda Fide' in Rome, which trained missionaries. He died of influenza while ministering to the Roman populace. He was chosen as patron of pharmacists in 2006.

In England and Ireland

Blessed John Henry Newman, Priest

Optional Memorial

Blessed John Henry Newman (1801-1890) was born in London, educated at Trinity College, Oxford and embarked on a highly successful career as a Fellow of Oriel College and Vicar of the University Church of St Mary's. A prominent member of the Oxford Movement, he became a Catholic in 1845; soon afterwards, he was ordained priest and introduced the Congregation of the Oratory into England. He lived at the Birmingham Oratory, continuing his ministry as a pastor, writer and educationalist, and in 1879 was created Cardinal Deacon of San Giorgio in Velabro by Leo XIII. He was beatified by Pope Benedict XVI in 2010.

In England

10 October

Saint Paulinus of York, Bishop

Optional Memorial

St Paulinus (+ 644) was one of the second band of missionary monks sent from Rome to assist St Augustine of Canterbury in 601. After labouring for many years in Kent, he was consecrated first bishop of York in 625 and did much to evangelise Northumbria, baptising King St Edwin at Easter 627. He was eventually driven from York and spent his final years administering the See of Rochester.

In Ireland

11 October

Saint Canice, Abbot

Optional Memorial

St Canice or Kenneth (c.525-600), one of the 'Twelve Apostles of Ireland,' was born in Glengiven in Derry and spent a period in Wales under St Cadoc. After a visit to Rome, he returned to Ireland and founded several monasteries, including Aghaboe in County Laois. He also worked energetically in Scotland, bringing many to the faith.

In England

12 October

Saint Wilfrid, Bishop

Optional Memorial

St Wilfrid (c.634-c.710) was educated at Lindisfarne and spent some years in Rome. He was a strong proponent of Roman observances, especially at the Synod of Whitby (664). He took charge of the new monastery at Ripon and became Bishop of York, although quarrels with the king and the Archbishop of Canterbury led to his exile and five years of missionary work in Sussex, the Isle of Wight and Friesland. He was buried at Ripon and his body later translated to Canterbury.

In England

13 October

Saint Edward the Confessor

Optional Memorial

St Edward (c.1005-66) was the son of King Ethelred 'the Unready' and spent nearly thirty years as a political exile in Normandy, his mother's homeland. He succeeded as King of England in 1042 and was subsequently famed for his life of prayer, chaste marriage and love of the poor. He built St Peter's Abbey in Westminster, where he and most of England's monarchs are buried.

14 October

Saint Callistus I, Pope and Martyr

Optional Memorial

St Callistus (+ 222) was a former slave who became Bishop of Rome in 217. He fought heresy and preached God's mercy for repentant sinners, despite meeting the criticism of 'rigorists' such as Tertullian. He is perhaps best remembered for the Roman catacomb that bears his name, where many of the victims of anti-Christian persecution were buried. St Callistus himself is venerated as a martyr, although the manner of his death is uncertain.

15 October

Saint Teresa of Jesus, Virgin and Doctor of the Church

Memorial

St Teresa (1515-1582) was born in Avila (Spain). She joined the Carmelite convent at Avila and, after a quarter of a century as a nun, began to reform the Order, with the help of St Peter of Alcántara and St John of the Cross. She founded seventeen reformed houses in Spain and, despite her busy life of administration, reached the highest 'mansions' of union with God. Her outstanding works of ascetical and mystical theology led her to be declared a Doctor of the Church in 1970.

16 October

Saint Hedwig, Religious

Optional Memorial

St Hedwig or Jadwiga (c.1174-1243) was born at Andechs (Germany) into a princely and saintly family; indeed, her niece was St Elizabeth of Hungary. Aged twelve, she married Henry the Bearded, later to succeed as Duke of Poland, and bore him seven children (including Henry the Pious and Konrad the Curly). She led a life of piety and solicitude for the poor and the sick and, in her widowhood, retired to the Cistercian monastery of Trebnitz, which she had founded.

Saint Margaret Mary Alacoque, Virgin

Optional Memorial

St Margaret Mary Alacoque (1647-1690) was born at Verosvres in Burgundy (France) and joined the Order of the Visitation at Paray-le-Monial. She received mystical revelations concerning the Sacred Heart of Jesus and, with the help of her Jesuit confessor, St Claude de la Colombière, spread this devotion throughout the world. She was canonised in 1920.

In Wales

Saint Richard Gwyn, Martyr

Optional Memorial

St Richard Gwyn (c.1537-1584) was born in Montgomeryshire (Wales) and spent many years working as a schoolmaster. A married man with six children, he was imprisoned for four years because of his Catholic faith and finally hanged, drawn and quartered at Wrexham on 15 October 1584. His last words were 'Iesu, trugarha wrthyf', 'Jesus, have mercy on me'.

In Ireland

Saint Gall, Abbot and Missionary

Optional Memorial

St Gall (c.550-640) was born in Leinster and joined the Abbey at Bangor. He accompanied one of his teachers, St Columban, on his missionary journey to Gaul and helped establish churches and monasteries. He eventually separated from his master and settled in what is now Switzerland, where an important monastery was dedicated to him and was renowned for centuries as a centre of learning; its library is still world-famous.

17 October

Saint Ignatius of Antioch, Bishop and Martyr

Memorial

St Ignatius (+ c.107) followed St Peter as bishop of Antioch and was thrown to wild beasts in Rome (possibly at the Colosseum) during the persecution of Trajan. On his way to Rome he wrote seven epistles, which give a clear picture of Christian belief and practice a century or so after Christ's birth. His name is mentioned in the Roman Canon.

18 October

Saint Luke, Evangelist

Feast

St Luke (first century) was a Greek, possibly from Antioch, who trained as a doctor. He converted to Christianity, became a disciple of St Paul and wrote both a Gospel and the Acts of the Apostles. His vivid descriptions of the childhood of Jesus have led some to surmise that he was close to the Blessed Virgin Mary. He is believed to have died in his old age, and may have been martyred; he is patron of doctors and artists.

19 October

Saints John de Brébeuf and Isaac Jogues, Priests, and Companions, Martyrs

Optional Memorial

St John (Jean) de Brébeuf (1593-1649), St Isaac Jogues (1607-46) and their six companions were Jesuit missionaries, originally from France, who dedicated their lives to preaching the Gospel among the indigenous peoples of North America. St John de Brébeuf was captured by the Iroquois, fastened to a stake, tortured to death and then partly eaten, near Midland, Ontario (Canada). St Isaac Jogues had already suffered slavery and mutilation during his missionary work, but returned to Canada from France. He was seized by the Mohawks, who thought he was a sorcerer, and tomahawked to death near Auriesville, New York in 1646.

Saint Paul of the Cross, Priest

Optional Memorial

St Paul of the Cross (Paolo Francesco Danei) (1694-1775) was born in Piedmont (Italy) and, following a spiritual conversion, founded a congregation of missioners with a special devotion to the Lord's passion and death (the Passionists). The first house was founded on Monte Argentario and, despite facing many problems, there were twelve Passionist 'Retreats' (community houses) by the time of his death, as well as a community of nuns. He had a special interest in England and regularly prayed for its conversion.

23 October

Saint John of Capistrano, Priest

Optional Memorial

St John of Capistrano (1386-1456) was married in his youth but it was later annulled. He gave up a promising career in order to join the Franciscans and became a popular preacher in Italy and beyond, often being entrusted with papal missions. He preached a crusade after the Turks captured Constantinople in 1453 and exhorted the victorious Christian troops at the battle of Belgrade in 1456. He died shortly afterwards of the plague at Ilok (Croatia).

24 October

Saint Anthony Mary Claret, Bishop

Optional Memorial

St Anthony Mary Claret (1807-1870) was born near Barcelona (Spain). In 1849 he founded the Missionary Sons of the Immaculate Heart of Mary (Claretians) and was appointed Archbishop of Santiago (Cuba). He worked hard to spread the Gospel and ensure better conditions for slaves. Such was the anti-clerical mood that no less than fifteen attempts were made on his life. In 1857 he returned to Spain and acted as confessor to Queen Isabella II.

In Wales

25 October

Six Welsh Martyrs and their Companions

Feast

The Feast commemorates six Welsh martyrs: St Richard Gwyn (c.1537-1584), St John Jones (c.1559-1598), St John Roberts (c.1575-1610), St Philip Evans (1645-1679), St John Lloyd (c.1630-1679) and St David Lewis (1616-1679). These stand as representatives of the many who suffered persecution during the sixteenth and seventeenth centuries, and risked their lives for love of the Church and the Holy Eucharist.

In England

26 October

Saints Chad and Cedd, Bishops

Optional Memorial

These two brothers were monks of Lindisfarne who became bishops in the seventh century. St Cedd (+ 664) founded an abbey at Lastingham, North Yorkshire, and became bishop of the East Saxons. St Chad (+ 672) succeeded his brother as Abbot of Lastingham and became Archbishop of York. Although, due to a dispute, he was removed from office by St Theodore, he was allowed to continue his episcopate in the Midlands, fixing his residence at Lichfield. His relics are now preserved at St Chad's Cathedral, Birmingham.

In Ireland

27 October

Saint Otteran, Monk

Optional Memorial

St Otteran or Odran (+ c.548) who may have been British by birth, was an associate, possibly a kinsman, of St Columba. Irish tradition makes him abbot of Meath and founder of Lattreagh. He worked on Iona and helped bring the Gospel to the people of Scotland. He is the principal patron of the Diocese of Waterford.

28 October

Saints Simon and Jude, Apostles

Feast

St Simon (first century) is usually called 'the Canaanite' and 'the Zealot', suggesting he belonged to the Jewish party of the 'Zealous of the Law'.

St Jude or Thaddeus (first century) has a short epistle in the New Testament ascribed to him, and is popularly invoked as the patron of hopeless causes.

Tradition says that after Pentecost they evangelised, Simon in Egypt, Jude in Mesopotamia, and then together in Persia, where they were martyred. Their names appear in the Roman Canon.

In Ireland

29 October

Saint Colman, Bishop

Optional Memorial

St Colman (c.550-632) was born at Corker in Kiltartan and, after leading the eremitical life on Aranmore and in the mountains of County Clare, he became Abbot and bishop of Kilmacduagh. He is said to have had a close affinity with animals: a cockerel woke him for the night office, a mouse kept him awake, and a fly marked his place on the page.

NOVEMBER

1 November
All Saints
Solemnity

The Solemnity of All Saints celebrates all those who are in Heaven, in the light of God's face – both those recognised by the Church as saints and those known only to the Lord. We ask for their intercession and we strive to follow their example, so that we too can fulfil our vocation to be saints.

2 November
The Commemoration of all the Faithful Departed (All Souls' Day)

Having celebrated the saints in Heaven, the Church today turns her attentions to the Holy Souls in Purgatory – holy because Heaven awaits them but suffering the pain of purification in the crucible of God's love. It is customary for priests to celebrate three Masses on this day for the Mass, the sacrifice of Calvary renewed on our altars, has always been the principal means of fulfilling the great commandment of charity towards the dead. The process of purgation can also be assisted through our prayers, penances and good works. Today we are reminded that the love which we have for one another in this world is stronger than death.

3 November
Saint Martin de Porres, Religious
Optional Memorial

St Martin de Porres (1579-1639) was born in Lima (Peru), the illegitimate son of a Spanish nobleman and a former slave. He became a Dominican lay brother and was exemplary in his care for the sick, his love of the poor and his devotion to the Blessed Sacrament.

In England and Wales
Saint Winifride, Virgin
Optional Memorial

St Winifride or Gwenfrewi (seventh century) was the niece of St Beuno. According to legend, despite making a vow of chastity, she was courted by Caradoc, son of a local chieftain; eventually he decapitated her. However, her uncle restored her to life and she ended her days as a nun at Gwytherin (Wales). For centuries pilgrims have visited her shrine and well at Holywell, the site of her attempted murder.

In Ireland
Saint Malachy, Bishop
Memorial

St Malachy (1094-1148) was brought up in Armagh and was ordained priest at the age of twenty-five. In 1123 his uncle, who was a lay abbot, gave him the abbey of Bangor, which he rebuilt. Soon afterwards he became bishop of Connor and, in 1132, Archbishop of Armagh. He reformed the Church, made sure the liturgy was everywhere celebrated according to Roman models and, after stepping down from office, made two pilgrimages to Rome. He was a friend of St Bernard, whose foundation at Clairvaux he greatly admired; although the famous 'prophecies' regarding future popes often attributed to him are in fact a product of the seventeenth century.

4 November
Saint Charles Borromeo, Bishop
Memorial

St Charles Borromeo (1538-1584) was born into a noble family at Arona, on the shores of Lake Maggiore (Italy). His uncle was Pope Pius IV and this ensured his quick promotion within the Church; aged only twenty-one he was created Cardinal Priest of Santa Prassede, although he was only ordained when in 1564 he became Archbishop of Milan. He zealously applied the teachings of the Council of Trent to his diocese, establishing seminaries and schools and renewing the life of the clergy. During the plague of 1576 he was active in the care of the sick.

In Wales

6 November
Saint Illtud, Abbot
Optional Memorial

St Illtud or Illtyd (+ c.505) is claimed as a disciple of St Germanus of Auxerre. He founded the great monastery of Llanilltud Fawr (Llantwit Major) in Glamorgan (Wales), which produced many saints. An early source calls him 'the most learned of the Britons in both Testaments and in all kinds of knowledge.' Later legends have him born in Brittany, which is possible if unlikely.

In Ireland

All the Saints of Ireland
Feast

Ireland, especially in the early Christian centuries, was known as an isle of saints and scholars. Many of these combined pastoral care with observance of the monastic life. The Irish also did much to bring the faith to other parts of Europe and, if we are to believe the story of St Brendan, even further afield.

In England and Ireland

7 November

Saint Willibrord, Bishop

Optional Memorial

St Willibrord (658-739) was originally from Northumbria and was educated at Ripon under St Wilfrid. He dedicated his life to preaching the Gospel in northern Europe, becoming Archbishop of the Frisians in 695 and setting up his residence at Utrecht (Netherlands). He also founded a monastery at Echternach (Luxemburg), where his relics are venerated.

In Wales

8 November

All Saints of Wales

Feast

This Feast commemorates the hundreds of Welsh saints recognised by the Church across the ages, as well as those known only to God. Many of them date from the so-called 'Age of the Saints' in the fifth and sixth centuries and often have connections with the Christian communities in Cornwall, Ireland, Scotland and Brittany.

In Scotland

Blessed John Duns Scotus, Priest

Memorial

Blessed John Duns Scotus (c.1265-1308) was probably born at Duns in the Borders (Scotland), joined the Franciscans and studied at Cambridge, Oxford and Paris. 'Scotist' thought had a great influence on medieval philosophy and theology. Among other achievements, the 'Subtle Doctor' is remembered for his strong defence of Our Lady's Immaculate Conception, at a time when many doubted the dogma. He died in Cologne and was beatified by Blessed John Paul II in 1992.

9 November

The Dedication of the Lateran Basilica

Feast

The Basilica of St John Lateran is the Cathedral of Rome, built under Constantine and consecrated by Pope Sylvester in 324. The Feast of its dedication rightly honours 'the mother and mistress of all churches of Rome and the world' and renews our union with and love for the See of Peter.

10 November

Saint Leo the Great, Pope and Doctor of the Church

Memorial

St Leo the Great (+ 461), a son of Tuscany, became Pope in 440. Though unable to attend the Council of Chalcedon in 451, his letter (or Tome) defining Christ's twofold nature was acclaimed as the Church's teaching: 'Peter has spoken through Leo.' His famous meeting with Attila the Hun outside

Rome the following year saved the city from destruction then, although, despite his efforts, it was pillaged by Vandals in 455. Leo's theological writings earned him the title of Doctor of the Church.

11 November
Saint Martin of Tours, Bishop
Memorial

St Martin (316-397) was born to pagan parents at Szombathely (now Hungary, but then in the Roman province of Pannonia) and served as a soldier. At the age of eighteen he was baptised and, around this time, met a naked beggar to whom he gave half his cloak. That night he had a dream in which the Lord Himself was wearing his cloak. St Martin founded a monastery and became Bishop of Tours (France). He was one of the first saints to be popularly venerated despite not being a martyr.

12 November
Saint Josaphat, Bishop and Martyr
Memorial

St Josaphat (c.1580-1623) was born in Volodymyr-Volynskyi (Ukraine) of Orthodox parents, though he later became a Catholic and entered the Basilian Order at Vilnius. As Archbishop of Polotsk, he worked faithfully for the reform of the Church and unity between East and West. He faced much opposition and suffered martyrdom at the hands of an angry mob at Vitebsk (Belarus).

In Wales

14 November

Saint Dyfrig, Bishop

Optional Memorial

St Dyfrig or Dubricius (+ c.550) may have been born at Madley, Herefordshire (England). According to tradition, he became a bishop, founded several monasteries and educated the likes of St Samson and St Teilo. We can probably discount Geoffrey's of Monmouth's claim that Dyfrig crowned King Arthur. He eventually retired to Bardsey Island, where he died in the middle of the sixth century and where his relics were venerated until they were translated to Llandaff Cathedral in 1120.

In Ireland

Saint Laurence O'Toole, Bishop

Optional Memorial

St Laurence O'Toole (1128-80) was born near Castledermot, County Kildare, and entered the monastic life after spending a period as hostage in the hands of a rival chieftain family. At the age of twenty-five he was chosen as Abbot of Glendalough and in 1161 became Archbishop of Dublin. He lived simply and returned to Glendalough every Lent. However, much of his time was occupied with ecclesiastical reform and negotiations with the English. He died while travelling through Normandy in 1180 and was buried at Eu.

15 November

Saint Albert the Great,
Bishop and Doctor of the Church

Optional Memorial

St Albert the Great (1206-80) was born in the Swabian town of Lauingen (Germany) and studied at Padua and Paris. He became a Dominican and taught theology; his pupils included St Thomas Aquinas. In 1260 he was appointed bishop of Regensburg but resigned two years later and returned to academic pursuits. The encyclopaedic breadth of his writings earned him the title of 'Universal Doctor' and patron of students of the natural sciences.

16 November

Saint Margaret, Secondary Patron of Scotland

Optional Memorial (In Scotland: Feast)

St Margaret (1046-93) was the granddaughter of King Edmund Ironside of England but was born while in exile in Hungary. In 1070 she married King Malcolm III of Scotland and had eight children, three of whom reigned as Kings of Scotland, including St David I. Remarkable for her piety and works of charity, St Margaret co-founded Dunfermline Abbey and organised ferries at North and South Queensferry for pilgrims crossing the Firth of Forth on the way to St Andrews. She is the secondary Patron of Scotland.

Saint Gertrude, Virgin

Optional Memorial

St Gertrude (1256-c.1302) was born in Eisleben (Germany) and joined the Benedictine convent at Helfta. She showed great talent in her philosophical and literary studies but is best known for her mystical writings. She had a marked devotion to the Holy Souls in Purgatory and to the Sacred Heart of Jesus, which later developed into its modern form with the visions of St Margaret Mary.

In England
Saint Edmund of Abingdon, Bishop
Optional Memorial

St Edmund (c.1175-1240) was born in Abingdon (England) and studied at Oxford and Paris. He lectured for a time at Oxford, before becoming treasurer at Salisbury and then, in 1233, Archbishop of Canterbury. With the help of a strong team, which included St Richard of Chichester, he did much to reform ecclesiastical discipline and defend the rights of the Church. He died in 1240 at Soisy (France), while on his way to Rome, and was buried at nearby Pontigny. He gave his name to the Order of St Edmund, founded at Pontigny in 1843, and Colleges at Oxford, Cambridge and Old Hall Green in England.

---

17 November
Saint Elizabeth of Hungary, Religious
Memorial (In England: Optional Memorial)

St Elizabeth (1207-31), daughter of King Andrew II of Hungary, was born at either Sárospatak (Hungary) or Bratislava (then Hungary, now in Slovakia). She married Ludwig IV, Landgrave of Thuringia (Germany), and had three children. St Elizabeth was widowed at the age of twenty and devoted herself to the poor and the sick. She founded a hospital at Marburg and was a Third Order Franciscan.

In England

Saint Hilda, Religious

Optional Memorial

St Hilda (614-680) was born into the Northumbrian royal family and baptised by St Paulinus at the age of thirteen. She eventually decided to enter the religious life, aged thirty-three, and became superior of the double monastery (men and women) at Hartlepool. She later moved as Abbess to the double monastery at Whitby, where she hosted the famous Synod in 663-64 which reconciled the differences between Roman and Irish usages. St Hilda died in 680 and her supposed relics were in later years claimed by Glastonbury and Gloucester.

In England

Saint Hugh of Lincoln, Bishop

Optional Memorial

St Hugh (c.1140-1200) was born at Avalon in Burgundy (France) and first entered the Augustinian Canons, before moving to the stricter Carthusian Order. After ten years at the Grande Chartreuse, he was sent to Witham in Somerset (England) to take charge of the recently-founded Charterhouse there. In 1186 he was reluctantly appointed Bishop of Lincoln and proved to be a holy and reforming pastor. He died at his residence at Lincoln's Inn, London, in 1200 and his symbol is a swan, a reference to the swan of Stowe that became his companion and guarded him as he slept.

18 November

The Dedication of the Basilicas
of Saints Peter and Paul, Apostles

Optional Memorial

The dedication of these two major basilicas allows us to express our communion with the Church in Rome. Both basilicas were completed in the fourth century and commemorated the two great Apostles: St Peter's on the Vatican Hill was built above the tomb of the first Pope and St Paul's outside the Walls was likewise erected over the final resting place of the Apostle of the Gentiles.

21 November

The Presentation of the Blessed Virgin Mary

Memorial

The Presentation of Mary in the Temple as a young girl is based not on the New Testament but on an account in the apocryphal Gospel of James. In being presented in this way, the Blessed Virgin dedicated herself to the service of God and kept herself open to God's will. The feast prepares us for Advent and Christmas, when we celebrate the coming of her Divine Son into the world.

22 November

Saint Cecilia, Virgin and Martyr

Memorial

St Cecilia (third century) was a Roman martyr. Legend makes her a noblewoman who founded a church in Trastevere, Rome, and was martyred under Marcus Aurelius – when attempts to suffocate her in the bathroom failed, a headsman was sent to decapitate her. However, three strokes failed to severe her head and she lingered on for three further days, praying and singing to God. She is mentioned in the Roman Canon and venerated as patron of music.

23 November

Saint Clement I, Pope and Martyr

Optional Memorial

St Clement (+ 97) was the third pope after St Peter and author of a famous letter to the Corinthians, an early example of the bishop of Rome's universal jurisdiction. Tradition records him being sentenced to hard labour in the Crimea and thrown into the sea, tied to an anchor (his emblem in art).

Saint Columban, Abbot and Missionary

Optional Memorial (In Ireland: Memorial)

St Columban (c.540-615) was born in Leinster (Ireland) and entered the monastic life at an early age. With a dozen companions he travelled to the continent and founded many monasteries in France and Italy, including Luxeuil and Bobbio, although his strict discipline sometimes aroused opposition. He died at Bobbio in 615.

24 November

Saint Andrew Dũng-Lạc, Priest, and Companions, Martyrs

Memorial

The feast celebrates the witness of 117 Vietnamese martyrs, who died between 1625 and 1886 and were canonised in 1988. They include St Andrew Dũng-Lạc (1795-1839), a Vietnamese diocesan priest who was beheaded at Hanoi in 1839. Twenty-one of the martyrs were foreign missionaries, such as St Théophane Vénard, a member of the Paris Society of the Foreign Missions, who was beheaded in 1861 and exercised a strong influence on St Thérèse of Lisieux.

25 November
Saint Catherine of Alexandria, Virgin and Martyr
Optional Memorial

St Catherine of Alexandria was a fourth century martyr. Later tradition makes her a well-born maiden of Alexandria (Egypt) who was martyred after refusing to worship pagan gods. During her interrogation, she ably defended the faith in a debate with the city's leading philosophers. According to legend, her body was taken by angels to Mount Sinai, where a monastery was built in her honour.

In Ireland
Saint Colman, Bishop
Optional Memorial

St Colman (c.530-c.606) was born in Munster and acted as a bard at the royal court of Cashel. He was a mature convert to Christianity, supposedly baptised by St Brendan, ordained priest and eventually consecrated as first bishop of Cloyne.

In Ireland
27 November
Saint Fergal, Bishop and Missionary
Optional Memorial

St Fergal (Ferghil, Vergil or Virgil) (+ 784) was an Irish monk, possibly educated at Colbroney under St Samthann and going on to become Abbot of Aghaboe. Like many Irish monks, he set off on his 'pilgrimage for the love of Christ' in 723, passing through France and southern Germany and eventually being appointed Abbot of St Peter's, Salzburg and then bishop. Despite several disagreements with St Boniface, St Fergal did much to build up the Church in Salzburg and elsewhere; he is remembered as Apostle of the Slovenes. He also had a keen interest in mathematics and astronomy.

30 November

Saint Andrew, Apostle and Martyr, Patron of Scotland

Feast (In Scotland: Solemnity; In England: Feast)

St Andrew (first century) was born at Bethsaida and worked as a fisherman. He is called the Protokletos or 'first called', for he was originally a disciple of St John the Baptist before following Christ and bringing with him his brother, St Peter. After Pentecost he zealously preached the Gospel and was crucified at Patras (Greece). He is the Patron of Scotland, where his relics were formerly venerated at St Andrews.

DECEMBER

3 December
Saint Francis Xavier, Priest
Memorial

St Francis Xavier (1506-1552) was born near Pamplona in what is now Spain and studied in Paris, where he became a follower of St Ignatius Loyola. A founding member of the Society of Jesus, he tirelessly brought the Gospel to India, Borneo, Indonesia and Japan. He died of fever on Shangchuan Island in 1552 while travelling to China.

4 December
Saint John Damascene, Priest and Doctor of the Church
Optional Memorial

St John Damascene (c.657-749) was born in Damascus (Syria), already under Muslim rule, and became a monk in the monastery of St Sabbas, near Jerusalem. He wrote many theological works and hymns, including 'The day of Resurrection'. He is considered the last Eastern Father of the Church; he was declared a Doctor of the Church in 1890.

6 December
Saint Nicholas, Bishop
Optional Memorial

St Nicholas (fourth century) was born perhaps at Patara (now in Turkey) and became bishop of Myra. He may have been imprisoned under the Emperor Diocletian and have attended the Council of Nicaea which opposed the Arian heresy. He is venerated in both the East and the West, especially as a patron of sailors and of children, as can be seen in the Christmas tradition of 'Santa Claus'. The saint's relics were later brought to Bari (Italy).

7 December
Saint Ambrose, Bishop and Doctor of the Church
Memorial

St Ambrose (c.340-397) was born in Trier (now in Germany, but then capital of the Roman prefecture of Gaul) and worked as a lawyer. In 370 he was appointed Governor of Liguria and Aemilia, with a residence in Milan. In 374 he was chosen to be the city's bishop, much to his surprise – not only was he a layman, but he was also not yet baptised: he was a catechumen preparing for baptism. He proved to be an outstanding bishop, not afraid to challenge the actions of the emperor and uncompromising in his struggle against Arianism. His converts included St Augustine and his teachings have led him to be numbered as one of the Latin Doctors of the Church.

8 December
The Immaculate Conception of the Blessed Virgin Mary
Solemnity

Today we celebrate the Blessed Virgin's unique privilege of being preserved from the stain of sin at the very moment of her conception. This was fitting for she would one day carry the second person of the Trinity in her womb. Blessed John Henry Newman wrote that 'there is no difference in kind between her and us, though an inconceivable difference of degree. She and we are both simply saved by the grace of Christ.' But with Mary, the manner in which she was saved was exceptional: from the first moment of her existence, she was freed from the stain of Original Sin. This dogma was solemnly defined by Blessed Pius IX on 8 December 1854 but had long been believed by Christians.

9 December
Saint Juan Diego Cuauhtlatoatzin
Optional Memorial

St Juan Diego (1474-1548) was born near what is now Mexico City and converted to Christianity in middle age. He showed a great piety and walked many miles to attend Mass. While doing so on 9 December 1531, the Blessed Virgin appeared to him on Mount Tepeyac, asking that a shrine be built on the spot. The local bishop asked for a sign and Our Lady left a miraculous portrait of herself on St Juan Diego's tilma or mantle.

In Wales

10 December
Saint John Roberts, Priest and Martyr
Optional Memorial

St John Roberts (c.1575-1610) was born in Trawsfynydd in Gwynedd (Wales), educated at St John's College, Oxford and joined the Benedictines, making his novitiate at San Martin, Santiago de Compostela (Spain). He alternated between working on the English Mission and spending time on the continent, where he became first Prior of St Gregory's, Douai, a house for English Benedictines that later moved to Downside

Abbey, Somerset. He was captured on a number of occasions and eventually hanged, drawn and quartered at Tyburn on 10 December 1610.

---

11 December

Saint Damasus I, Pope

Optional Memorial

St Damasus (c.304-384) was probably born in Rome, although his father, a priest, may have been originally from Spain, leading to stories that Damasus too was born there. He was ordained a deacon and eventually became Pope in 366. He proved to be a strong leader, promoting devotion to the martyrs and their relics, strengthening the administration of the Church and summoning synods and councils to counter heresy.

12 December

Our Lady of Guadalupe

Optional Memorial

On 9 December 1531 the Blessed Virgin Mary appeared to St Juan Diego and left an image of herself imprinted upon his cloak. The image was placed in a magnificent shrine at Guadalupe where it became an object of great devotion and encouraged the devotion of the Mexican nation towards the Mother of God. Many miracles were attributed to her intercession and Our Lady of Guadalupe was named as 'Queen of Mexico and Empress of the Americas'.

In Ireland

Saint Finnian, Bishop

Optional Memorial

St Finnian (+ 549) was probably born at Idrone, County Carlow, and spent some time in Wales learning the monastic way. Back in Ireland, he founded many churches and monasteries, including the one at Clonard, County Meath, and his disciples were so numerous that he was known as the 'Teacher of the Saints of Ireland.' He is said to have died in 549 while nursing victims of the plague.

13 December

Saint Lucy, Virgin and Martyr

Memorial

St Lucy (+ c.304) was probably born in Syracuse (Sicily) and martyred during the persecution of Diocletian. Legend makes her the daughter of a wealthy family who was brought up as a Christian, and, having resisted the advances of a pagan suitor, was arrested, tortured and killed. Her name is mentioned in the Roman Canon and her feast, situated near the shortest day of the year, is celebrated in Sweden and elsewhere as a festival of light.

14 December

Saint John of the Cross, Priest and Doctor of the Church

Memorial

St John of the Cross (1542-91) was born in Fontiveros (Spain) and entered the Carmelites. He befriended St Teresa of Avila and was persuaded to lead the reform of the Order, though he subsequently suffered many tribulations, including imprisonment at the hands of his brethren. A renowned poet and mystic, he wrote much on the mystery of the Cross and the 'dark night of the soul'.

In Ireland

18 December

Saint Flannan, Bishop

Optional Memorial

St Flannan (seventh century) was, legend tells us, the son of a chieftain, who made a pilgrimage to Rome and was consecrated bishop by Pope John IV. Whatever the truth of this, he may reasonably be reckoned the first bishop of Killaloe. He also preached in the Hebrides; the uninhabited Flannan Isles, west of Lewis and Harris, are named after him.

In Ireland

20 December

Saint Fachanan, Bishop

Optional Memorial

St Fachanan (sixth century) is a saint of whom little is known for sure. He probably founded a monastery at Kilfenora, County Clare, and is venerated as its first bishop and patron. The Diocese of Kilfenora was later joined to that of Galway.

21 December

Saint Peter Canisius, Priest and Doctor of the Church

Optional Memorial

St Peter Canisius (1521-97) was born in Nijmegen (Netherlands) and joined the Society of Jesus. He worked mostly in central Europe, becoming known as the 'second apostle of Germany,' and energetically promoted the aims of the Catholic Reformation. Among his many works, the "German Catechism" was particularly influential. He spent his final years in Fribourg (Switzerland), where he founded a school.

23 December

Saint John of Kanty, Priest

Optional Memorial

St John Cantius (1390-1473) was born at Kanti or Kanty near Cracow (Poland). He spent most of his life lecturing in Cracow, though for a time he was pastor of Olkusz. He was distinguished for his piety and love of the poor, with whom he shared his earnings.

26 December

Saint Stephen, the First Martyr

Feast

St Stephen (+ c.35) the Proto-martyr was one of the seven deacons who assisted the Twelve, 'filled with faith and with the Holy Spirit' and 'full of fortitude'. Denounced to the Jewish authorities as a blasphemer, he was stoned to death outside Jerusalem. He died praying for those who killed him; present at his martyrdom was Saul of Tarsus, soon to become the Apostle of the Gentiles.

27 December

Saint John, Apostle and Evangelist

Feast

St John (+ c.100) was the son of Zebedee and worked as a Galilean fisherman with his brother St James. He was called while mending his nets to follow Jesus and became 'the disciple whom Jesus loved'. Alone among the Twelve, he stood at the foot of the cross and was entrusted to the Blessed Virgin. He wrote the fourth Gospel, three Epistles and the Apocalypse, producing profound passages on such themes as the divinity of Christ and the centrality of love. Though tradition records his attempted martyrdom 'at the Latin Gate' in Rome, St John lived to a great age, spent many years in exile on Patmos and finally died in Ephesus.

28 December

The Holy Innocents, Martyrs

Feast

The Holy Innocents were the young children of the neighbourhood of Bethlehem, all under the age of two, put to death by Herod in an attempt to kill the Infant Jesus. Some ancient texts number the victims in the thousands but in all probability there were no more than two dozen. On this Feast of 'Childermas', while still in the Christmas Octave, these innocent, nameless victims are honoured as the first to shed their blood for Christ.

29 December

Saint Thomas Becket, Bishop and Martyr

Optional Memorial (In England: Feast)

St Thomas (1118-1170) was born in Cheapside, London and rose to become Henry II's Chancellor and (from 1162) Archbishop of Canterbury. His episcopal consecration sparked off a religious conversion; he changed from being 'a patron of play-actors and a follower of hounds to being a shepherd of souls'. His final years were dedicated to defending the rights of the Church, which led to disagreements with the king and resulted in six years of exile. Shortly after returning to Canterbury, he was murdered by agents of the king in his own cathedral on 29 December 1170. St Thomas was canonised three years later and is honoured as patron of the pastoral clergy in England.

31 December

Saint Sylvester I, Pope

Optional Memorial

St Sylvester (+ 335) was a Roman who succeeded St Miltiades as Pope in 314, shortly after the Edict of Milan granted toleration to Christians. Alongside these new freedoms and the building of magnificent new churches, St Sylvester had to deal with the heresy of Arianism and sent representatives to the great Council called at Nicaea in 325. He was one of the longest reigning popes (nearly 22 years) and one of the first non-martyrs to be venerated in Rome. His relics are now preserved at San Silvestro in Capite.

INDEX

Index of Saints

A

C

H

I

J

A History of the Papacy

Over its 2000-year history, the papacy has lived the full range of human experience, including war, murder and exile. The Popes themselves have at times been men of vision and zeal – true saints – and at other times scheming politicians and great sinners; yet the institution founded by Christ himself has survived. This extraordinary booklet surveys the changing role of the Supreme Pontiff, giving an overview of the many ways it has affected the spiritual and temporal history of the world, starting with the Galilean fisherman right up to Pope Benedict XVI.

Fr Nicholas Schofield is a Parish Priest and Archivist of the Archdiocese of Westminster. He has co-written The English Cardinals and The English Vicars Apostolic and writes a history column for The Catholic Times.

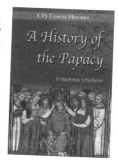

ISBN: 978 1 86082 672 6

CTS Code: H 510